THE HEART
OF CHRISTIAN
LEADERSHIP

Learning to Lead with the Character of Jesus

Dedicated to my wife, Loice, whom God has used more than she will ever know to shape my character and to help me be the leader I am today.

THE HEART OF CHRISTIAN LEADERSHIP

Learning to Lead
with the Character of Jesus

JON BYLER

LeadersServe
www.LeadersServe.com

The Heart of Christian Leadership
By Jon Byler

Copyright © 2010 Jon Byler

3rd edition 2014
ISBN-10: 0-9770085-1-7
ISBN-13: 978-0-9770085-1-3

Published by
LeadersServe
www.LeadersServe.com

Previously published by
Global Disciples, Lancaster, PA. USA
and Authentic Books, India

Unless otherwise noted, "Scriptures are taken from the HOLY BIBLE, NEW INTERNATIONAL VERSION. Copyright © 1973, 1978, 1984 International Bible Society. Used by permission of Zondervan Bible Publishers."

Cover photo by Elizabeth with Joseph Byler

TABLE OF CONTENTS

Introduction   9

Part One: The Foundation

1. The Heart of the Matter   13
2. The Leader and Servanthood   23
3. The Leader and Brokenness   43
4. The Leader and Motives   57

Part Two: Building on the Foundation

5. The Leader and His Tongue   67
6. The Leader and Truthfulness   83
7. The Leader and Authority   101
8. The Leader and Forgiveness   127
9. The Leader and Family   149
10. The Leader and Transition (Leaving Well)   163
11. The Leader and Endurance (Finishing Well)   173
    Epilogue   193
    Recommended Books/Resources   195
    Bibliography   199
    About the Author   200

1 Corinthians 13 for Leaders

If I speak with words that excite the crowd and bring me lots of praise, but have not love, I am no better than a politician making noise. If I have the gift of leadership and can galvanize people around my vision; if I have the latest leadership advice from the experts at my fingertips but have not love, I am an empty shell of a man. If I learn to serve others and stoop to do the most menial jobs, but have not love, my heavenly account is in the hole.

True leaders are patient when followers just can't see the big picture, they have time to listen to the small child who will not make a bit of difference on their monthly report, they are not jealous of the explosive growth of their neighbors' church, and they don't publicize their own successes.

Christ-like leaders don't brush others off, even when their diary shows an important meeting coming up; they don't make decisions based on how it will look on their resume; they don't blow up even when a staff member makes a stupid mistake that makes him look bad, and he doesn't write it down in a record book.

Servant leaders aren't happy when they hear negative reports about others, but rejoice when they hear that someone is succeeding. Leaders worth their salt defend the weak they are leading, they risk trusting even after they have been stabbed in the back, they keep believing in people through the darkest times and they never give up. The pure heart of a genuine leader never falters. Books, seminars, and the latest management techniques will fail, homiletical masterpieces will be destroyed in the shredder, degrees will wrinkle and fade away. Even the best leaders only know a part of the whole, but when Christ returns, he will fill the gaps.

Immature leaders try hard, but are a poor reflection of the master. But when he returns, he will lead us perfectly. Real leaders constantly recognize that one day they will look Jesus in the eye and account for their leadership. Then their eyes will be fully opened. Meanwhile, leaders keep leading with faith in God, hope for a better future, and love for those they lead. But the greatest of these is love.

INTRODUCTION

What does it take to make an effective Christian leader? Many Christians, including myself, wrestle with this question. I don't pretend to have all the answers, but allow me to share my leadership journey with you.

By age 21 I knew God had called me into full time Christian ministry and I began to prepare for that work. I attended college and graduated with a degree in Christian Ministries. By God's grace I sensed that my beautiful certificate had not adequately prepared me for my life's work, so I worked for a year as an apprentice to an experienced church planter. Working with him, I received practical experience, but I was still a novice in leadership. In 1991, I moved to Kenya, East Africa where I was assigned to pastor a newly planted church. For the next five years I gave my heart and soul to that work, making my share of mistakes and enjoying some successes as well. I was committed to building the people of God. I loved them and opened my heart to them. I encouraged leaders to develop and spent time deliberately training others to do the work of ministry. I learned about setting goals, preparing a budget, and many other practical issues of leadership. I taught my leaders through a Theological Education by Extension (TEE) training program and seminars, hoping to see them mature in Christ and continue leading the church.

Our church grew from 30 people to 250 and we were able to plant two other churches during that time. As I led the church, I was also called to be an overseer and for several years I worked with 15 churches in the region. As I experienced the joys and frustrations of these leaders, I began to wrestle with a lot of questions about leadership. I longed to see all of the churches doing well and growing strong, but some weren't. Of course the pastors would give nice testimonies about how God was blessing their churches, but when I visited I saw only the same faces that I'd seen the year before! What was happening? What could be done to strengthen these churches? Why were some growing and others not growing? I thought the answer lay in **education**. *If only these pastors could go to Bible school,* I thought, *things would change.* So I encouraged them to attend Bible schools. For some it helped; for others it seemed to make things worse! My question remained unanswered.

Next, I considered the **environment**. Some of the pastors lived in difficult localities, where the people were poor or uneducated, and perhaps this made it impossible to grow the church. Then a close friend of mine, who had no theological training, traveled to a remote location to start a church. Within a few years he had a strong church and had even begun planting others! Another of my theories proved unfounded!

Meanwhile, I continued to pour my life into leaders. I taught at a part-time Bible school, started a TEE program in the church, held leaders' seminars and regularly met and prayed with the pastors I was overseeing. Many of my questions, however, remained unanswered. I nearly concluded that some people can be leaders and that others will just never make it in leadership. It appeared to be a sovereign decision by the Almighty God over which I had no control.

During this period, I was called to work with the Centre for Christian Discipleship (CCD), a ministry devoted to equipping leaders. I started reading and studying more about leadership and was particularly challenged and influenced by materials from Rev. John Maxwell. He taught me that "everything rises and falls on leadership" and that leaders are not born, but that they are made.[1] His words gave me fresh hope that leadership can be learned and he provided practical resources and ideas that have shaped my teaching since that time. Thank you Rev. Maxwell!

I began again with renewed vigor and a fresh determination to make a difference in the lives of leaders. For the next six years I was

---

[1] John C. Maxwell, *Developing the Leader Within You* (Nashville, TN: Thomas Nelson, 1993), viii, 1.

involved in training leaders through the Leadership Training Institute and different programs connected with CCD.

As I reflect now on what it takes to make an effective Christian leader, I have identified three essential components: character, knowledge and leadership skills. These three components are like the three legs of a stool.

> Three essential components of Christian leadership: character, knowledge and leadership skills.

Each leg is necessary for the stool to stand properly and without one of them the stool is very unstable. Without knowledge of the Bible a leader will not be able to communicate truth effectively and he will not be able to draw on the vast resources contained in the Scripture to strengthen him as a leader. But, the acquisition of Bible knowledge without character will create an arrogant leader who will not be able to sustain his leadership over time. The effective leader also needs to have knowledge about what leadership is as well as knowing his/her own stregths and weaknesses. Some leaders have both knowledge and good character, but still are not effective leaders. They lack the third "leg"— leadership skills. They are wonderful people to be around and they love God deeply, but their churches will never grow to their full potential because they are not good leaders.

Leadership skills include the ability to connect well with people, to possess and communicate vision effectively, to set goals and manage time well, to understand many different types of people, to equip and release others, to possess administrative and communication skills, and to perform many other functions. We can also think of these components as the head, the heart and the hands. David, the shepherd king, combined all three in a powerful and effective way. With his *head* he knew God, to the extent that he was called a man after God's own heart (see 1 Samuel 13:14). The Bible also says of him; "And David shepherded them with integrity of *heart*; with skillful *hands* he led them" (Psalm 78:72 italics mine).

In my ministry God has called me to focus on the latter two "legs" of the three-legged stool: character and leadership skills. This focus does not in any way imply a lack of respect for those whom God has called to devote their lives to equipping leaders with knowledge. I thank God for what they are adding to the lives of leaders.

This book focuses on character. The companion book, *The Art of Christian Leadership*, focuses on leadership skills. Both are written for those in leadership or aspiring to leadership positions. The principles shared in this book are applicable to Christian leaders in all spheres of society including the church. As you read, I pray that it will be useful in your life, making you a more effective leader in the church, in your home and in society.

This book should be used first of all for personal study. Read, reflect and respond. Use the action assignments at the end of each chapter to allow the material to change your life. And after it has changed you, use it to teach others!

This book grew out of classes that I have taught to students striving to improve their skills as leaders and to develop their character. I have co-written Chapter 8 with my wonderful wife, Loice Byler, and the final chapter with my mentor and friend, Ken Stoltzfus. The chart on p. 54 is used with permission from Johnny Long. Special thanks go to those who helped me prepare this manuscript including Florence Muchami, Linda Moffet, Amy Calkins, and Linda Boll. What a gift each of you have been to me!

Chapter One

THE HEART OF THE MATTER

Think with me for a moment of a leader that you greatly admire. Why do you respect that person? Why are you drawn to that person? Don't read further until you have answered these questions in your mind.

What is your answer? Did you think of his/her appearance? Did you consider their academic achievements? Not very likely. Did you think of things that he does (actions) or did you think of inner qualities (character) that he possesses? Most likely you thought of that person's character traits rather than his credentials or behavior. If you did think of actions, recognize that these actions flow out of character. Character is normally what draws us to certain leaders and repels us from others.

Think about Nelson Mandela, a leader who is respected all over the world. What gives him such great influence in the lives of so many? Is it because he was in a position of leadership? No, for many years he held no position except as a prisoner! Mandela is highly respected because of his character, his ability to endure imprisonment without bitterness, his desire for peace instead of conflict and his willingness to forgive those who had so deeply wronged him. He is an outstanding leader because of his character.

What is character? Simply put, it is *the qualities or traits that make up a person.* It is the core of your being, the heart of who you are. Reputation is who others think you are; character is who you actually are.

The Importance Of Character

God looks for character

This world emphasizes external credentials. When you apply for a job, you must produce a resumé or curriculum vitae that shows what you have accomplished academically or professionally. We judge an individual's success by the extent of his material possessions. We judge a pastor, not by the size of his character, but by the size of his congregation. We judge a businessman by his quarterly earnings rather than what happens in his heart.

God, however, looks past all of those things and goes straight to the heart. 1 Samuel 16:7 says:

> But the LORD said to Samuel, 'Do not consider his appearance or his height, for I have rejected him. The LORD does not look at the things man looks at. Man looks at the outward appearance, but the LORD looks at the heart'.

Again and again, when God wanted a leader, He chose the person of character rather than competence. He was not interested in diplomas or academic achievements. He scanned the crowd for people with pure hearts. 2 Chronicles 16:9 says, "For the eyes of the LORD range throughout the earth to strengthen those whose hearts are fully committed to Him."

Scripture refers to David as a leader after God's own heart (Acts

13:22). He accomplished great successes in leadership but also failed in several significant areas. Yet, his heart was right before God. He possessed a solid character. He knew and fully embraced the importance of repentance and humility before God.

In his book, *Spiritual Leadership,* J. Oswald Sanders writes, "Our Lord made clear to James and John that high position in the Kingdom of God is reserved for those whose hearts—even in the secret places where no one else probes—are qualified."[2]

When God looks at your heart, what does He see? Does He see a man or woman of God?

Followers look for character

Not only does God look for character, but followers also look for character in leaders. People all over the world are crying out for leaders with good character. The world landscape is littered with leaders who have devoted their lives to accumulating power and wealth for themselves at any cost. Integrity is daily sacrificed on the altar of convenience. The masses are groaning inwardly and longing for a man or woman of character to stand up and lead.

Henry Clay stated, "Of all the properties that belong to desirable men, not one is so highly prized as that of character."[3] His statement is a reflection of the writer of Proverbs who said, "A good name is more desirable than great riches; to be esteemed is better than silver or gold" (22:1).

Character in a leader produces confidence in followers, who will more willingly adopt the leader's vision. Myles Munroe writes, "The only way for others to have confidence in you is to see that you are faithful over little things, committed to your purpose, and willing

---

[2]J. Oswald Sanders,*Spiritual Leadership* (Chicago: Moody Press, 1994), 19.
[3]Henry Clay, *Text-Book of Eloquence, a Collection of Axioms, Apothegms, Sentiments ... Gathered from the Public Speeches of Henry Clay*, ed. G. Vandenhoff (n.p., 1844), 93.

to die for your cause."[4] Without this confidence and trust, effective leadership is impossible. Maxwell calls trust the *indispensable quality* of leadership, saying, "Leadership only functions on the basis of trust."[5]

When your followers look at you, do they see a person of character, a person they can trust?

Character determines our success in Christian leadership

Character is the foundation of successful Christian leadership. Leadership is influence and the ability to influence others is closely linked to character. Rick Renner says, "Your influence is only as strong as your personal life."[6] Without solid character, long-term success in leadership is impossible. You can build short-term success on charisma and charm, but you cannot build a lasting work for God without solid character.

Munroe states, "The quality of your character is the measure of your leadership effectiveness. True leadership cannot be divorced from the basic qualities that produce good sound character."[7] Many Christian leaders have risen on the wings of success only to crash suddenly because of a character flaw.

For some, the issue has been greed, for others, immorality, or rebellion against authority; but in each circumstance, the issue relates to the leader's character. Some leaders have the ability to rise to the top but lack the character to remain there. Character determines how far you will go, how long you will go and how many will go with you.

For this reason, many leaders fail despite their quality education and extensive Bible knowledge. They may even possess well-developed

---

[4] Myles Munroe, *Becoming a Leader, Everyone Can Do It* (Bakersfield, CA: Pneuma Life, 1993), 83.

[5] John Maxwell, "Leadership That Goes the Distance," *Leadership Wired* 3, no. 9 (April 2000): 1.

[6] Rick Renner, *Who is Ready for a Spiritual Promotion?* (Tulsa, OK: Rick Renner Ministries, 2000), 90.

[7] Munroe, *Becoming a Leader, Everyone Can Do It*, 115.

leadership skills. But sooner or later, character flaws will be exposed and cost them the respect of their followers. Lack of character always carries a high price. The writer of Proverbs wisely said, "Above all else, guard your heart, for it is the wellspring of life" (4:23). An anonymous writer said it this way: "When wealth is lost, nothing is lost. When health is lost, something is lost. When character is lost, all is lost." Character is the heart of leadership.

The Development Of Character

Since character is indispensable in the life of a leader, you must think carefully about how your character is developed. Character development is a lifelong process that requires continual work.

Unfortunately, reading books or attending classes does not develop character. Even a book like this one that focuses on character cannot give you a good character; it can only provoke you to make choices that will build your character. Your personal character development rests in your own hands, and it requires hard work. James Froude, the British historian, said, "You cannot dream yourself into a character; you must hammer and forge yourself one."

For this reason, teaching character development is extremely difficult. It is much easier to teach knowledge and leadership skills than to teach character. Nevertheless, it is helpful to look at several ways in which our character is developed.

Character is developed through our daily choices

Maxwell writes, "Talent is a gift, but character is a choice."[8] You face thousands of choices daily. You make many insignificant choices about which clothes to wear or what to have for lunch. But you also make thousands of choices daily that determine your destiny and shape

---

[8]John C. Maxwell, *The 21 Indispensable Qualities of a Leader* (Nashville, TN: Nelson Business, 1999), 4.

your character. You choose to speak the truth or to lie; you choose to respond in anger or in love; you choose to forgive or to become bitter. God, through the Holy Spirit, is eager to continually work on your character. You have the power to choose whether you will submit with increasing obedience to His voice or whether you will ignore His promptings and walk in your own way.

As I reflect on my life, I remember several times that I made character choices that have significantly shaped my life. On one occasion, I was working as a carpenter on someone's house. As I worked, I noticed a beautiful fruit tree in the yard. After several days of admiring the fruit, I decided to sample it and discovered that it was good.

I finished the job and went to other places. Later God began to remind me that I had taken something that belonged to someone else without permission. The Bible calls that stealing. I wrestled, thinking up all kinds of excuses for why I didn't need to go and confess my sin to the owner. "It was just a small issue," I told myself. Furthermore, "I'm sure the owner would have allowed me to eat if I had only asked!"

After days of internal struggle, I made the choice to go and admit what I had done. The pain of that step shaped my character and forever took away my appetite for stolen fruit. It was a choice that developed character in me. I could have chosen the easy way out, dulled my conscience and lived the rest of my life in mediocrity. But I wanted to grow in Christ-likeness, so I paid the price of honesty and made the right choice.

At other times, I chose to deal with broken relationships instead of running away, to admit sins of my tongue to those I had wronged and to discipline my mind to learn the word of God when I could have been relaxing. All of these choices shaped my character. No one else could make those choices for me; I had to do it myself. In this way, leaders must impose upon themselves a self-discipline that will allow God to shape character in their lives. As Munroe states, "True leaders cultivate character with the fertilizer of self discipline."[9]

What choices did you make in the last week that shaped your character? More importantly, what choices do you need to make today in order to build a better character for tomorrow?

Character is developed through difficulties

Let's face it, when everything is going well, having the right attitude and doing the right things is easy. But character develops when you go through difficult times of suffering or testing. In fact, nothing reveals character like times of testing. When pressure is applied to your life, you find out who you really are. Like a lemon, which only releases its bitter juice when squeezed, you will exhibit your true nature when squeezed by hard times.

Difficult times not only reveal who you are but also provide opportunities for you to grow in character. Paul, writing to the believers in Rome, said, "Not only so, but we also rejoice in our sufferings because we know that suffering produces perseverance; perseverance, character; and character, hope" (Romans 5:3-4). Knowing that God can redeem the difficult things of life in ways that will shape your character allows you to rejoice in hardship. Too often, you cry out to God for relief from your circumstances instead of discerning what God wants to teach you through them. Those who labor through the difficult times with God will develop character.

Character is developed through time

Solid character is not the fruit of a moment but of a lifetime. Character is not received through the laying on of hands or through attending a one-day seminar. There are no shortcuts to building character; it requires time.

When God wanted to train Moses, He took him to the wilderness for 40 years. Joseph labored 13 years in slavery before he was ready to lead a nation. David spent years as a fugitive hiding from King

---

[9] Munroe, *Becoming a Leader, Everyone Can Do It*, 162.

Saul before God was ready to use him. Jesus invested three years into shaping the lives of the disciples. Paul waited three years in the desert before God used him to lead the church.

What was God doing? He was building character. Just because Moses had the passion to kill an Egyptian didn't make him ready to lead the nation. Joseph was not ready to be a leader simply because he had a dream.

> "Reputation is made in a moment: character is built in a lifetime."

He needed to learn some tough lessons and make the choices that would correctly shape his character. God took years teaching David to wait on His timing and to submit to even an ungodly authority.

Character development takes time. Someone said, "Reputation is made in a moment: character is built in a lifetime." You must be patient. And patience itself is only developed through a time of waiting. When you impatiently demand that God develop you quickly, you still lack a crucial element of character – patience.

This is why Paul cautions Timothy, "Do not be hasty in the laying on of hands, and do not share in the sins of others" (1 Timothy 5:22). Paul knew that promoting a person to a position of leadership before his heart was ready would produce disastrous results. This is where many young people fail. They feel called and anointed of God for ministry but they don't realize that their character is not yet fully developed. Instead of being discouraged, they should acknowledge the immaturity of youth and focus on developing their character while they are young.

When God produces a cabbage, He takes three months; when He produces a hardwood tree, He takes over 50 years. Which type of person would you rather be?

This, then, is the formula for character development:

Right Choices + Difficulties + Time = Character

Welcome to God's school of character development!

ACTION ASSIGNMENT:

1. Take some time alone and evaluate your life. What character flaws can you identify? List them on paper and develop a plan to work on them. *wanting appreciation too much sometimes, listening, communication, unthankfulness*

2. What choices do you need to make right now in your life that will strengthen your character? *try to ask clarifying as to grow listening comm. skills & spend time giving thanks*

"Take care of your character and your reputation will take care of itself."

Chapter Two

THE LEADER AND SERVANTHOOD

Many different kinds of leaders exist in the world and they practice many different types of leadership. Some leaders seek to please people and they change philosophies every time the political wind changes direction. Others seek their own personal gain, financial gain or prestige, and care little what others think. Some genuinely care about the people under them; others completely fail to care. Some leaders talk and communicate; others dictate. Some willingly get their hands dirty and help with the work; others simply give orders and watch the work.

A glance at Christian leaders also reveals many different types of leaders. Some function as "benevolent dictators." Some focus on building their own kingdom, regardless of the cost. Others genuinely desire to meet the needs of their followers. What kind of leaders does God want? Should you lead like the leaders of the world? In this chapter, I will discuss the answer that Jesus gave on the last night of His earthly ministry.

> Also a dispute arose among them as to which of them was
> considered to be greatest. Jesus said to them,
> "The kings of the Gentiles lord it over them; and those who
> exercise authority over them call themselves Benefactors.
> But you are not to be like that. Instead, the greatest among
> you should be like the youngest, and the one who rules
> like the one who serves. For who is greater, the one who
> is at the table or the one who serves? Is it not the one who
> is at the table? But I am among you as one who serves"
> (Luke 22:24-27).

This conversation took place between Jesus and His disciples during an intimate final evening together. They had walked together for three years. The disciples had watched Jesus perform mighty miracles; they sat in the front row of all of His "seminars" and listened to every word that He spoke. They felt excited and expectant – something big was about to happen. The previous Sunday they had watched all of Jerusalem shout "Hosanna" as Jesus entered on a donkey. Jesus Himself had spoken of coming events and the disciples sensed that His ministry was nearing a climax.

What did they expect? The disciples were convinced that Jesus was the Messiah, come to reign on David's throne. They believed, like most of their contemporaries, that the Messiah would overthrow the political enemies of Israel and establish a kingdom greater than King David's.

When you understand their expectations, it is easy to imagine how the disciples hoped to gain personally through Jesus' rise to power. Jesus was going to be a king, and everyone knows that a king needs assistants to help rule. No president governs without a cabinet; no commander without generals. And who would be the natural candidates for key positions in Jesus' administration? The disciples, of course. No wonder, then, that as they ate their roasted lamb their conversation turned to their future positions.

Jesus seized the opportunity, however, to give His disciples a leadership lesson. He first denounced worldly leadership and then described what He expected from His own leaders.

Jesus Denounces Worldly Leadership

Jesus made it clear that there are two ways to lead: His way and the way of the world or the "Gentiles." Obviously He wanted His disciples to follow His way instead of the world's way. This passage from Luke reveals three characteristics of the world's leadership.

Worldly leadership is concerned with position

The disciples were arguing. The Bible states it like it really was without trying to paint a beautiful picture of these 12 men. It would be nice to think that they were heatedly discussing the best strategy for reaching the world for Christ or splitting theological hairs about whether to baptize forwards or backwards. But no, they were debating over who was the greatest. They were concerned about who would sit in the coveted seats and dominate the new administration. They each wanted to prove themselves most worthy to be the vice president of the royal cabinet. They were ultimately concerned with positions.

Imagine their dialogue as they debated the issue. Maybe their conversation went something like this:

> **Peter**: (he was always the first to speak!)
> "There's no doubt in my mind that I'll be the greatest. I'm already the one closest to Jesus and have been called to be alone with Him several times. He already said that I'm the rock on which He will build His kingdom. And by the way, which of you walked on the water like I did?"
>
> **Andrew**: "My brother Peter, you're a great guy and we all know that you talk a lot. But I have one question for you, 'Who introduced you to Jesus?' I did! I know that

Jesus won't forget what I did in those early days. I was called before you and walked with Jesus before you did. That should tell you something about who is the greatest!"

Matthew: (the tax collector) "Hey guys, you're talking big tonight! Sure you joined early, but Andrew, remember what happened when Jesus called me? I invited all of you to my house and gave a banquet in His honor. You guys ate like you had never seen meat before! Which of the rest of you honored Jesus like that? Surely with my vast experience and great resources, He will appoint me to a top position in His administration. After all, the rest of you were just poor, uneducated fishermen!"

Judas: "Matthew, you're speaking like a wealthy man. It's true you had money before Jesus called you but who has the money now? When you all want to go out on any journey, who do you ask for money? Everyone knows that the man who controls the money is the most powerful man, and I am that man! I will be the greatest!"

James: "Wait a minute Judas. You might control the money but that doesn't make you close to Jesus. Remember when Jesus went up on the mountain? Did He choose you to go along? No, He took me! That should make it clear He considers me the closest friend."

Thomas: (The doubter) "I doubt if any of you are right! I don't think Jesus will even make it to be the king. When the Romans come with their mighty army we might all die as traitors."

John: (interrupts softly) "I don't know what this argument is all about. I didn't even want to say anything but it seems that you are all misguided. James, remember that you were not alone with Jesus on the mountain. I was also along. It was you and me and Peter that were called. The other time when we went with Him we saw Him raise the dead girl. It should be clear to any of us that the three of us are the closest to Jesus. But among the three of us, who is the greatest? Peter, what does Jesus call me? He calls me 'the one that I love!' Are any of the rest of you called anything like that? That should settle the argument once and for all!"

This argument occurred during the last supper of Jesus, immediately before the first Holy Communion. And this was not even the first time that they had argued like this (see Mark. 9:34). But now the tensions were higher. They needed to settle some issues before Jesus became the king. And each wanted the top position.

Among worldly leaders, position is everything. Who is on the top? Who is most important? Who can give orders to others? Who is number one and who is number two? Position determines greatness. In the political world, any time people shift positions, the newspapers spend days analyzing who is moving up and who is moving down, who is getting closer to the president and who is losing favor.

Worldly leadership is controlled by power

Notice then, what Jesus says, **"The kings of the Gentiles *lord it over* them . . . and *exercise authority . . .* "** or **"exercise lordship"** (Luke 22:25, KJV). Power and authority control worldly leaders. They enjoy leadership because it yields power. The leader commands others with his words. He speaks and others jump into action.

On the day of my wedding, I experienced the power of position. Especially during the reception I realized that if I wanted a soda, I didn't need to get money from my pocket and go to buy it. I just whispered to the person beside me, "A coke please" and someone went quickly. Soon the drinks appeared and I could even choose which kind I wanted. If I called for the photographer, he came running. I was in control; I had power and I must admit that it felt nice. Fortunately, by evening it ended, or it may have gone to my head!

Leaders in the world love to be in control and to exercise their power. They do not appreciate those who challenge or correct them. They desire leadership because it yields power and they will struggle and fight to get the positions that give them that power over others.

They live to give orders. In Africa, where I lived for 13 years, this is expressed in the 'chief mentality.' Every man thinks that he should be chief. How is this expressed in your culture?

Worldly leadership is consumed with prestige
Jesus says that these people like to be called "**benefactors**" (v. 25). A benefactor is someone who supports another person financially.

Worldly leaders like to claim this good name so that other people will notice them, recognizing and respecting their services to society. They love watching people bow down before them. Leadership gives them prestige.

Worldly leadership has many "perks" or privileges. A leader is able to get the best seat, drive a nice car and have the best piece of meat at the banquet. Leadership brings prestige.

> People in leadership often very sensitively guard their titles.

Titles are a sign of prestige. People in leadership often very sensitively guard their titles. The bigger the title, the better. Being called, "Your Worship, the mayor" or "Chairman" or "the Honorable…", or "Headmistress" or "Administrator", etc., bloats a person's ego.

A story is told of the former president of Uganda, Idi Amin. One day a Jewish captive tried to address him. With all respect he started, "Mr. President…" Idi Amin interrupted sternly, "My name is Field Marshall, Dr., Idi Amin, Da Da!" He wanted his title to be clear.

These three things mark worldly leadership: position, power and prestige. Notice, however, what Jesus says, **"But you are not to be like that"** (v.26). Jesus' kingdom contains a different standard for leadership, a different set of rules and a different code of values.

Instead of holding to this different standard, however, the person appointed to a position of Christian leadership often immediately adopts the patterns of the world. After all, this standard was modeled to him during his childhood, or in his experience with the church, and he unconsciously assumes that position, power and prestige are the essentials of leadership. Unfortunately, then, the three characteristics of worldly leadership often dominate the church as well. Think with me for a moment.

What about *position*? Pastors climb the denominational ladder, working hard in one church in hopes of being promoted to a bigger one. They frame the certificates that indicate their status. They vie for the seat next to the bishop at meetings. They carefully watch who is being promoted in the denomination and who is losing their position, forming alliances accordingly.

In the church, the members also struggle over position. "I think the women's committee is more important than the youths' because they have more money." "I am more important than the usher because I'm on the church council." "I am the chairman of the committee, so I am the highest." "Did you see who the pastor chose to give a testimony?" "Last year I was an usher, this year a deacon, next year an elder?"

What about *power*? Pastors often expect people to follow just because they have a position of power. They don't want their ideas to be challenged. They surround themselves with "yes" men who will unquestioningly support their ideas.

Members quickly get a taste of the power of leadership. "Did you see how people responded when I called for money to be given? They gave! That is power!" "What do you mean questioning what I am doing? Don't you know that I am the *chairman* of this committee?" "I'm the one who makes decisions about the money and I said that there's no money!"

What about *prestige*? "Hey, people call me "Mr. Chairman" or "Secretary" or one of the "elders" of the church. "Oh, people call me "Pastor" and it makes me feel so good." (In fact if you don't call him Pastor, he may not pray for you with passion!) Many churches have adopted special titles like, "the very Reverend", "the most Reverend", "the right Reverend" and many others.

Yes, often these characteristics of worldly leadership that Jesus condemns find their way into our lives as Christians. Can you see any of these characteristics in your own leadership? Are these characteristics evident in the world of business, art, and educational leadership? Allow Jesus' words to sink deeply into your heart, *"You are not to be like that."*

Jesus Describes Christian Leadership

After clarifying that He doesn't want His leaders to be like the leaders of the world, Jesus gives a positive description of what His leaders should look like.

Christian leadership is not concerned with seniority

Jesus says, "The greatest among you should be like the youngest" (v. 26). Jesus reverses the way we naturally relate. He says let the "most reverend" or the "CEO" become like the youngest member.

In families, the oldest receives respect. In many cultures, the oldest child has unquestioned authority. By virtue of his age, he can pretty well demand what he wants. "Bring this; do that," he says, and it must be done. In fact, in many cultures, an unwritten hierarchy determines importance and power according to age. Any person who is older can command those who are younger. The youngest person has no rights and can tell no one what to do, except maybe the chicken or the dog.

But Jesus commands leaders to become like the youngest. You must humble yourself and take the lowest position. Remember the disciples' argument about who was the greatest? Jesus says that you should not even worry about who is the greatest. You are not to think about whether or not you are the head of the committee. You should not be concerned about whether or not you are the chairman or the pastor. You are a brother or sister in Christ. When you become concerned with power and position, then you have lost sight of Christian leadership. Concerning names and titles, Jesus has some hard words:

> But you are not to be called "Rabbi," for you have only one Master and you are all brothers. And do not call anyone on earth "father", for you have one Father, and He is in heaven. Nor are you to be called "teacher," for you have one Teacher, the Christ. The greatest among you will be your servant. For whoever exalts himself will be humbled, and whoever humbles himself will be exalted (Matthew 23:8-12).

In Christian leadership there is no seniority or power struggles for names and titles.

Does this mean that it is always wrong to use titles or to have positions in the church or your organization? I do not think Jesus is against positions. But He warns against seeking positions. He recognizes the danger that creeps in when we start using titles and special names. It is not wrong to have a "pastor" or a "chairman" and to call him what his position reflects. It is good and healthy for followers to show appropriate respect for their leaders.

The danger comes when the person in the position demands or expects the title and believes himself greater than others because of it. Every organization should show honor to its leader. But if the leader comes and demands, "Where is my special chair?" he has not understood Jesus' teaching.

The disciples believed that greatness was connected with position, power and prestige. Jesus taught that greatness is, instead, rooted in our character.

Christian leadership is characterized by service
Jesus goes on to say, **"the one who rules [should be] like the one who serves"** (v. 26). The leader is to be like the one who serves. This

is radical. In your natural self you want to *be* served. You want others to do for you. You want to simply sit and enjoy the meal and let someone else worry about cooking and cleaning the dishes.

> Being a servant leader will change the way you lead others.

You want to let someone else worry about cleaning the building and setting up the chairs. You can so quickly feel, "I am too important for all of that." This is true of all people, but especially as you rise in a position of leadership, you will very quickly begin to believe that you are too high to serve.

But Jesus says that His leaders must be servants. Please hear what He is saying to you as a Christian leader today. You are the servant of the organization you lead. ***You are not the boss, not the dictator, but the servant. If you are not willing to be a servant, you are not qualified to be a Christian leader!***

Serving means **giving**, not **getting**. You lead to give to others, to bless them, to build them up and to strengthen them, not to gain the power, position or prestige that comes with leadership. As a leader you undoubtedly have influence and power. *The question is, "How will you use your influence and power? Will you build your own kingdom and name or will you build His Kingdom and His name?"* Paul speaks of his authority in 2 Corinthians 13:10, "the authority the Lord gave me [is] for building you up, not for tearing you down." Paul recognized that God entrusted authority to him for the purpose of building others, not for himself. You can lead in order to give and to build others, or to get for yourself and to tear down others. If you want to build Christ's Kingdom and His name, you must be a servant. As J. Oswald Sanders asserts:

> True greatness, true leadership, is found in giving yourself in service to others, not in coaxing or inducing others to serve you. True service is never without cost. Often it comes with a painful baptism of suffering. But the true spiritual

leader is focused on the service he and she can render to God and other people, not on the residuals and perks of high office or holy title. We must aim to put more into life than we take out.[10]

The world says that "servant" and "leader" are opposites. Jesus says that you are to be a servant leader and He illustrated with His life that both can happen together. **Being a servant leader will change the way you lead others.** When work needs to be done, will you simply give orders or are you willing to serve? Are you willing to serve the food or do you demand to be served? Are you willing to sweep the floor or clean the toilets?

Four Characteristics Of A Servant

Let's think about what Jesus meant when he told His followers to be servants. What characterizes a servant? Thankfully, most people do not know from experience what it is like to be or have a slave. Think instead of the lowest possible job in your culture, a person who does work that is despised. What characterizes a servant?

A servant recognizes authority

A servant knows that he is not building his own kingdom but helping someone else. He does not talk back to the person in authority because he knows that he holds the lowest position. He knows that the supervisor must be obeyed and that if he refuses to recognize his supervisor's authority, he will soon be looking for another job.

In our leadership we also need to recognize the authority which is over us. We are not building our own kingdom but God's.

---

[10] Sanders, *Spiritual Leadership*, 15.

A servant has no rights

A servant doesn't demand his rights; he has none. He exists to do the master's will. Servants don't go on strike. Many workers organize themselves and go on strike, demanding better pay or better working conditions. But servants don't. Why? They don't have (or don't realize that they have) any rights. Their complaints are seldom heard. They are told, "If you don't like it, you can leave!"

We are not leaders to get things from people; we need to give up our rights and serve. Do we expect things from those under us? Do we get angry when we are not treated with respect?

A servant expects to work hard

A servant doesn't hope to rest and be comfortable. He expects to work, and to work hard. From early in the morning to late at night, a servant works diligently. Jesus said:

> Suppose one of you had a servant plowing or looking after the sheep. Would he say to the servant when he comes in from the field, "Come along now and sit down to eat?" Would he not rather say, "Prepare my supper, get yourself ready and wait on me while I eat and drink; after that you may eat and drink?" (Luke 17:7-8).

No one applies for a job as a servant expecting to have an easy job. Serving is hard work, but for a servant that is all that is expected.

Servant leadership is HARD work! If you're not ready for hard work, you are in the wrong place!

A servant does not expect recognition

A servant does not expect to be thanked and applauded for his wonderful work. He simply does his job. Jesus continued His teaching on serving with these words, "Would he thank the servant because he did what he was told to do? So you also, when you have done everything you were told to do, should say, 'We are unworthy servants; we have only done our duty'" (Luke 17:9-10).

At the end of the day, do we say "Thank you" to those who do menial tasks? Not often! Servants are expected to work hard without any appreciation.

How do you respond when your work is not recognized? Are you willing to keep working even if no one notices?

Think about how these four characteristics of servitude apply to servant leadership. If you lead as Jesus instructed you to lead, you will recognize authority over you. You will not demand your rights or struggle for better benefits and treatment. You will recognize that leadership is hard work and, as a result, you will be willing to work longer and harder than anyone else. You will not work to be recognized.

Take a moment to examine your life as you reflect on the role of a servant.

Hindrances To Servant Leadership

If you are like me, you realize that being a servant is not easy. In fact, **everyone wants to *have* a servant; no one wants to *be* a servant.** What keeps us from leading as servants?

Pride hinders servant leadership

Pride is likely the biggest hindrance to servant leadership. You can easily scorn the low position; you want to be the boss. You crave recognition. Power feels good. Titles feed your ego. You like when people serve you. But pride in the life of a Christian leader cannot work. **"God opposes the proud but gives grace to the humble" (1 Peter 5:5-6).** After Peter's argument in the upper room, he appears to have learned the lesson well and teaches that when we are proud, even God will oppose us. I believe that leaders are more severely tempted than followers and are more prone to pride when thrust into high positions and lifted up by people. You must ask God to deal with your natural pride.

Insecurity hinders servant leadership

Insecurity is one of the greatest hindrances to servant leadership. An insecure person cannot receive criticism. He cannot stoop too low because he fears what others will think of him. He cannot allow others to simply call him a name without a title because he is not confident in his ability to lead and relies upon that title to reinforce his position. He believes that visibly serving others will diminish his authority. If you find it difficult to be a servant, check for signs of insecurity in your life.

Interestingly, just before Jesus stooped to wash the feet of His disciples, the Bible records, **"Jesus knew that the Father had put all things under his power, and that he had come from God and was returning to God; so he got up..." (John 13:3-4).** Jesus was secure in His _power_, His _origin_ and His _destiny_. He felt no need to prove himself to people and could stoop down and serve them.

A lack of role models hinders servant leadership

The lack of positive leadership examples also hinders our ability to be servant leaders. Not many people have grown up under a servant leader; not many have followed or observed a flesh and blood example. This is especially true in parts of the world where the church is young. Ngiwiza Mnkandla, a pastor from South Africa, said,
"African leaders are like the male lion that kills its young males to protect its supremacy."[11] I hear similar stories from India and other parts of Asia as well and recognize that even in the West many have not seen good examples of servant leaders.

Although the lack of role models makes servant leadership difficult, it does not make it impossible. Jesus still stands as the example. Look

---

[11]Ngiwiza Mnkandla, _The Church Leader in Africa_, 4th Qtr. 2000.

at His example and begin to pattern your leadership after His. As you follow His example you will provide an example for a new generation of leaders who know how to serve. Break free from the

> "African leaders are like the male lion that kills its young males to protect its supremacy."

bondage of your past, and commit yourself to radically obey the example of Jesus Christ.

The Example Of Servant Leadership: Jesus

Jesus provides the perfect model. He was the greatest leader that the world has ever known and yet He came as a servant. He says, **"I am among you as one who serves"** (Luke 22:27). What a statement for the King of Kings and the Lord of Lords!

In John 13, we witness an example of Jesus' servant leadership. Imagine with me the scene in the upper room during Jesus' last night with His disciples. As the disciples entered the room, their feet dirty from walking, they looked for the servant to take care of their needs. But no servant stood ready by the water and towel. Peter and John had prepared the place well. The meal was ready. The water and the towel were placed by the door. The only thing they had forgotten was the servant.

As each disciple entered the room, he saw the need for a servant. He could smell his feet (and the feet of the others) and did not want to eat with dirty feet. But who would take the place of the servant? Peter could not think of it, since he was the greatest. Each disciple had an excuse as he walked silently past the water and towel. Who would wash their feet? Where was the servant? Who would stoop low enough to serve the others?

Jesus looked around at the disciples, realizing what was happening. He, more than the others, had every excuse to sit and be served. He was the master; He was the teacher; and He was the leader. But He got up from the table and headed towards the basin.

I imagine that the discussion at the table about who was the greatest trailed off in painful silence as the disciples realized what was happening. They saw Jesus walking deliberately towards the water. They watched in disbelief as Jesus removed His teacher's robe, wrapped the towel around His waist, picked up the basin of water and headed back towards the disciples.

Awkward silence filled the room. Half-chewed food remained in their mouths. Although each disciple had reasons for why he should not be the servant, they each knew that this scenario was totally wrong. Any of them could have done it, but certainly not Jesus. He was the boss, their leader. He was the miracle-working-anointed-man-of-God. Peter even tried to refuse, but it was too late. Imagine how they felt as the world's greatest leader stooped to serve them. The impact of that lesson never left their lives and it should sink as deeply into our spirits as well.

By washing their feet, Jesus set an example for all leaders to follow. He explains further in **Mark 10:45 "For even the son of man did not come to be served but to serve and to give his life as a ransom for many."** Jesus did not demand to *be* served but He served and expects us to do likewise. Surely we are not greater than Jesus.

Many people want to serve Jesus, but do not want to serve others. Yet the greatness of our leadership capacity is measured by our willingness to serve those who work under us. Rick Renner says, "If we're 'greatly anointed,' that means we're greatly anointed to serve. That's why God gives His Spirit to empower us – not so we can sit around and boast of our magnificent revelations."[12] Perhaps this is why the word "leader" is not used very often in scripture. Sanders notes, "The King James Bible uses the term leader only six times. More frequently, the role is called servant. We do not read about 'Moses, my leader,' but 'Moses, my servant.' And this is exactly what Christ taught."[13]

In the natural realm it seems like a person that serves others will be taken advantage of, not respected, and will, therefore, fail to become a truly great person. **But in the Kingdom of God, *servant leaders* make the greatest leaders.** Christ humbled Himself and became a servant. For that reason, Paul says, *"God exalted him to the highest place and gave him the name that is above every name, that at the name of Jesus every knee should bow…and every tongue confess that Jesus Christ is Lord to the glory of God the Father" (Philippians 2:9-11).* Clearly, Jesus received position, power and prestige by becoming a servant.

Listen to the advice given to King Rehoboam, when he was deciding what kind of a leader he would be: "If today you will be a *servant* to these people and *serve* them and give them a favorable answer, they will always be *your servants*" (1 Kings 12:7, italics mine). These wise advisors recognized that serving those you lead produces great loyalty and respect. Unfortunately, Rehoboam followed the ways of the world, refused to serve and lost the kingdom.

Peter learned this lesson well and later in life wrote: "Humble yourselves, therefore, under God's mighty hand that he may lift you up in due time" (1 Peter 5:6). Serve people. They will love you for it and God will promote you in due time. **In the Kingdom of God true power to influence comes as we serve.**

What kind of leader are you? Do you lead like the world or like Jesus? Are you a servant or a boss? Put this book down and get alone

---

[12] Renner, *Who is Ready for a Spiritual Promotion?*, 203.
[13] Sanders, *Spiritual Leadership*, 21.

with God. Allow Him to work in your heart. Where you have failed, confess it to Him and ask Him to give you the servant heart of Jesus.

> *Because we children of Adam want to become great,*
> *He became small.*
> *Because we will not stoop,*
> *He humbled Himself.*
> *Because we want to rule,*
> *He came to serve.*
>   – J. Oswald Sanders[14]

---

[14] Sanders, *Spiritual Leadership*, 16.

ACTION ASSIGNMENT
Luke 22:24-27

Answer the following questions as honestly as you can.

1. Rate yourself in the area of service. Put an "x" next to the statement which "<u>best</u>" describes you.

    _____ I never lead as a servant

    __✕__ I sometimes lead as a servant

    _____ I usually lead as a servant

    _____ I always lead as a servant

2. Think about the three areas that Jesus denounced: Position, Power, and Prestige.

In which area are you <u>most</u> tempted personally? *position*
(Don't say "none," you will always be tempted in at least one of these areas.)

Give one example of how you are tempted in that area.

I want to be seen as godly, even in times when I'm not putting effort towards nearing Jesus

3. In what specific areas of leadership do you find it most difficult to serve others? (For example, doing menial tasks for them, expecting proper titles, giving your time, etc.)

being the example I "want to be" I have a lot of need for growth. :)

4. Look at the three hindrances to serving (pride, insecurity, lack of role models). Which one most hinders you from serving?

5. Read John 13. Mark here when you have done it _____. What reasons for *not* washing their feet could Jesus have given?

How does Jesus' example challenge you?

6. Write one specific step you have taken as a result of this lesson.

Chapter Three

THE LEADER AND BROKENNESS

A glass falls to the floor and breaks into a thousand pieces. Instantly it becomes worthless and is discarded. In the natural world a broken item immediately decreases in value.

But in our spiritual lives, the opposite is true. The more broken we are the more useful we are in the kingdom. Broken leaders operate much more effectively than unbroken leaders.

What exactly is brokenness? It *is an absolute surrender to the Lordship of Jesus Christ, allowing His rule to be supreme*. It means the death of my selfish nature, which insists on doing things my way, and the acceptance of Christ's way as the best. In fact, the biblical term for what I am calling brokenness is ***death***. No one, however, wants to read a chapter titled, "The Leader and Death," so I've used the word brokenness. Luke records Jesus' teaching about brokenness in the following words:

Then he said to them all:
"If anyone would come after me, he must deny himself
and take up his cross daily and follow me. For whoever
wants to save his life will lose it, but whoever loses his life
for me will save it. What good is it for a man to gain the
whole world, and yet lose or forfeit his very self? If anyone
is ashamed of me and my words, the Son of Man will be
ashamed of him when he comes in his glory and in the
glory of the Father and of the holy angels." (Luke 9:23-26)

The Expectation Of Brokenness

In this passage, Jesus speaks of a depth of Christian experience
that few of His followers bother to consider. He speaks of a life of
total surrender to His lordship, a giving up of all that is most dear to
you, a sacrifice of your very life.

His teaching is so radical that we often dismiss it as a call aimed
only at a select group of His followers. But Jesus intends His message
for all of us. He said to "them *all*" and spoke of "*anyone* who would
come after me" and "*whoever*." Clearly He targets not just a select
group of people, but all of His disciples. He is speaking to everyone
who desires to follow Him. He expects every disciple to enter into
this experience of brokenness with Him. Jesus knew that this teaching
would not be popular. He did not expect (or receive) a big "amen"
from His disciples after saying, "deny yourself and lose your life." But
He did not shrink back from clearly expressing His expectations. If
you ignore Christ's mandate in this passage, you are guilty of cheap
discipleship.

Clearly, you feel less threatened when you hear the call of Jesus to
"Go into all the world and preach the gospel" than to accept this call
to be broken, to die to yourself and to give up your life. Your flesh
fights surrender at all costs. Still, the expectation of Christ remains.
Will you accept or reject His terms?

The Experience Of Brokenness

Let's go a little deeper into Jesus' teaching. What does He really mean by brokenness and death? How will you experience this in your own life?

Brokenness demands death

The first thing that Jesus teaches us is that brokenness demands death. He says, "Take up your cross." In modern society we know little about the cross. The only crosses we see are in religious symbols in pictures or in jewelry around someone's neck. We might look at this verse and conclude that Jesus uses the cross as a symbol for suffering. Indeed many people, when faced with a difficult experience, sigh and say, "This is my cross."

> If you truly want to be His disciple you must die!

But the disciples knew exactly what he meant. They knew that the cross serves only one purpose: DEATH. It certainly involved significant suffering, but death was the ultimate reason for hanging someone on the cross. *The cross is an instrument of death*. So Jesus says that if you truly want to be His disciple you must die. Brokenness and full surrender to His lordship require death.

Brokenness deals with self

What exactly must be put to death? Jesus is obviously not talking of our physical bodies. He still expects us to continue living for Him. Jesus is saying that the *self* in us must die. He speaks of His true disciple denying "him*self*" and forfeiting his "*very self.*"

What is the *self*? Scripture sometimes refers to it as the "flesh." Not my physical flesh, but that part of me that desires to control my own life. The essence of sin is self, or the desire to be in control. The prophet Isaiah understood this when he said, "We all, like sheep, have gone astray, each of us has *turned to his own way*; and the LORD has laid on him the iniquity of us all" (Isaiah 53:6, italics mine). Roy

Hession notes that at the center of "sIn" is a big "I."[15] It is self that says "no" to God when He tells me to forgive. It is self that makes excuses for sin in my life or tries to hide it. It is self that refuses to be open with another brother or sister, preferring appearances instead of true fellowship. Self rebels against God and justifies my actions and attitudes. Self believes in my own superiority, believes that my church, my organization, my culture, my theology is the best. Self uses leadership position for personal advantage; it self-righteously belittles others and condemns the sin in their lives. It is self that rejects correction and refuses to admit a mistake. Self demands its "rights" and will not bend for anyone.

Christians often say things like, "Oh, that's just the way I am"... "I can't love that person"..."I can't forgive that person"..."I can't really expect to stop being angry. After all, look at what that person did to me"..."I can't go and share with that brother"..."I can't greet so and so"..."I can't submit to that man, you don't know my husband..." *These statements are manifestations of self.* Jesus says that self must be broken. Self must die. You must take up your cross, die to self, and allow Jesus to control your life. You must surrender, putting to death the fighting spirit within you. You quickly defend yourself, making excuses for wrong attitudes and accusing or blaming others for your attitudes. *Jesus says that self must die!* If you want Jesus to completely fill you, this self must be completely broken.

You will experience the abundant Christian life only through this death. Many believers struggle through their Christian lives unnecessarily, outwardly saying, "Praise the Lord," but inwardly allowing self to take control.

Of course, most of the time, we refuse to label manifestations of self as sin. We have better names like "little problems", "small difficulties", or excuses like, "that's just the way I am". In reality we are living with envy, pride, bitterness, harsh words, anger, unforgiveness, jealousy,

---

[15] Roy Hession, *The Calvary Road* (Fort Washington, PA: CLC Publications, 1964) 21-22.

etc. We must learn to recognize the manifestations of *self* and we must be willing to call them *sin*!

Paul discusses the expressions of the sinful nature in Galatians:

> The acts of the sinful nature are obvious:
> sexual immorality, impurity and debauchery; idolatry and witchcraft; hatred, discord, jealousy, fits of rage, selfish ambition, dissensions, factions and envy; drunkenness, orgies, and the like. I warn you, as I did before, that those who live like this will not inherit the kingdom of God (Galatians 5:19-21).

Paul wrote this list of sins to believers and it serves as a strong challenge, demanding that you examine your life and honestly evaluate whether you live in any of the fruits of the flesh listed above.

You need to identify the sin in your life before you can enjoy the solution. Jesus does not offer a cure for your "little problems" but He offers a cure for *sin*. The blood of Jesus cleanses you of your sin – if you confess it. I pray for a revival of confession of sin, that we may all be purified and washed by the blood of Jesus, that our pride will be broken, that the self in us will die on the cross and that the life of Jesus may live among us in a new way.

This is true revival. Revival does not come through some magical outpouring of God's power; it comes as the fruit of broken and submitted hearts and lives. Revival comes as you and I yield to God and, as a result, receive His power. We question why God waits so long to answer our prayers. I believe we have become complacent in sin. We have excused broken relationships. We have insisted on being right. But this attitude will kill our spiritual life. Not only that, it will destroy the life of the church. We should stop praying for revival and ask God to break us instead. *Only then* will we experience revival.

Paul spoke as a broken man when he said, "I have been crucified with Christ and I no longer live, but Christ lives in me. The life I live in the body, I live by faith in the Son of God, who loved me and gave Himself for me" (Galatians 2:20). He instructs us further in Galatians 5:24, "those who belong to Christ Jesus have crucified the sinful nature with its passions and desires."

Many are not willing to pay the price for this kind of revival. But if you hope to see the Kingdom of God on earth, you must be willing to carry your cross, to let go of grudges, to forgive your brother or sister. You must go to someone and say, "Please forgive me for the way I have spoken about you." This is revival, and it will cost you everything. John says that only when you "walk in the light" will you have fellowship with God and with your brothers and sisters (1 John 1:6-7). You cannot have fellowship with God while you are angry with a brother.

Brokenness demands daily action

An initial brokenness or death happens when you surrender your life to Christ. But most likely your life still contains many areas that remain unbroken and, because brokenness is a daily process, you can potentially live an only partially surrendered life.

Jesus commands you to take up your cross "daily" and follow Him (Luke 9:23). Every day you will face tests to die to self. These tests will not come as you read your Bible, but as you meet other people. God uses other people to test your brokenness. Maybe He will use your harsh boss, a rude coworker, your spouse's unkind words, or a report of gossip spoken against you. Your response to these situations reveals whether or not you will continue to walk in brokenness. Defensiveness, anger, hurt feelings, self-pity and blame-shifting all indicate self-focus.

This deeper life of death is a daily choice. If tomorrow I become angry with my wife and refuse to admit my sin, I will not have fullness in Jesus until I repent.

You may easily believe that another person's violation of your rights excuses your anger and bitterness. But it does not. **God does not hold you accountable for what others do to you, but He holds**

you accountable for how you *respond* to what they do. Instead of looking at people as your enemies, begin to see them as agents of God intended to test your brokenness.

The Effect Of Brokenness

Brokenness will revolutionize your entire life. Brokenness releases Christ to work in and through you. Watchman Nee, in his classic book *Release of the Spirit* says that when the self is broken the Spirit is released. He likens the self to a shell surrounding the Spirit of God. As long as the self is there, the Spirit is confined. But when the self is broken the Spirit can burst forth.[16]

Jesus demonstrated brokenness in both His life and death. Jesus suffered great slander, but He did not get angry. People hated Him, but He did not hate them. Even when He felt tired, He did not become irritable. People misunderstood and misinterpreted His words, but He refused to defend Himself. He silently accepted false accusations. Jesus daily surrendered His life to the will of God and, therefore, continually received power from His Father.

> Being broken people releases Christ in us.

The cross, of course, most clearly demonstrates Jesus' death to self. Although He neither deserved or desired this death, Jesus submitted Himself in the garden, praying, "Not my will but yours be done" (Luke 22:42). In the same way, Christ calls you to imitate Him – to be broken for Him as He was broken for you.

Brokenness in the home

The most difficult place to practice brokenness is in your home, where you are most likely to show your true nature. At home you

---

[16] Watchman Nee, *Release of the Spirit* , reissue ed. (Richmond, VA: Christian Fellowship Publishers, 2000).

remove your nice "masks." At home your real self shows up, often in unpleasant ways. Would you like to have Jesus live with you for ten days as a silent observer of your every action? I doubt it.

When you live in brokenness at home, you will admit your mistakes. You will confess honestly, "I was wrong. Will you forgive me?" You will also know how to lovingly correct others. Many times, harsh words of correction toward your children or your spouse spring out of unconfessed sin in your own life. When properly broken, you will speak in love and discipline in love.

Further, when you are broken you will give up your "rights." You may believe you deserve a peaceful, quiet evening. A husband may feel that he has a "right" to have his meal every evening at the same time, or to be obeyed without question, even when his commands are foolish. A wife may feel that it is her "right" to be loved and cherished, or to have freedom to schedule her own life. All these "rights" produce conflict in Christian homes. We must remember that as servants, we possess no "rights." In true brokenness, yield your "rights" to God and learn to live peacefully, even when those "rights" are not met.

Brokenness in leadership

Brokenness also greatly affects your leadership. It enables you to receive criticism without becoming defensive. Leadership often provokes criticism simply because no leader can please everyone. How do you respond when someone challenges you? An unbroken leader becomes harsh and defensive, and often uses his power to silence opposition. A broken leader will carefully listen and closely examine the issue before responding. In the face of legitimate criticism, he will be secure enough to change and even to thank his critic. When criticism is unjustified, he will continue on his course while still expressing love to the concerned person.

The broken leader does not think too highly of himself. Although as a leader he may be extremely capable, his brokenness keeps him dependent on God. He recognizes that he needs both God and other people to help him be an effective leader.

A broken leader will not fear affirming and promoting others. Because he seeks to extend the Kingdom of God, and not his own, he rejoices in the successes of others, even when they exceed his own.

A broken leader is transparent with people. He refuses to hide behind walls of pretense and act like a "super saint" who never even thinks of sin. He deals gently with those who struggle because he admits his own struggles. He does not look down on others, but walks alongside them in humility. Even when his position demands that he take disciplinary measures, he acts with gentleness and love.

A broken leader serves others. He can do this without reservation because the issues of pride and self have been settled. The broken leader is secure in who he is and is not fighting for a position or trying to impress others. Jesus demonstrated this just before he stooped to wash the feet of his disciples. He was able to serve His disciples because He knew who He was and what His father had called Him to do. He had died to His own agenda and ambitions.

The world needs these kinds of leaders. Our homes need these sort of people. The church waits for men and women who will model Jesus' command to "die daily." Your school or business cries out for a broken leader. Are you willing today to die? Are you willing to give up the characteristics of self that are still in your life? Are you willing to say, "Jesus I need to be cleansed. I am carrying around a lot of self. I see it in my attitudes towards people, in the way I respond to authority, and in the way I respond to my spouse"?

Go ahead. Do it now. Allow Christ to break you and empty you of self. Then, and only then, will He be fully seen in you. Take some time alone with God, prayerfully reflecting on the teaching of this chapter. Complete the action assignment and open yourself to the work that God wants to do in your heart. Look at the differences between proud people and broken people. Honestly mark the statement on each line which best describes you right now. I pray that God will bring you to personal brokenness so that He can fully use you in His work.

ACTION ASSIGNMENT

1. Would you say that you have had a "breaking point" experience in your life?

   If so, describe briefly what happened and how it impacted your life and leadership. If not, what has kept you from it?

2. Reflect on the following scripture by answering the questions below:
   "I have been crucified with Christ and I no longer live, but Christ lives in me. The life I live in the body, I live by faith in the Son of God, who loved me and gave Himself for me" (Galatians 2:20). What does it mean to be "crucified with Christ?"

   To what extent have you experienced this verse in your own life?

   What practical things could you do to make your life more like this verse?

3. Slowly read the verses below.
   The acts of the sinful nature are obvious: sexual immorality, impurity and debauchery; idolatry and witchcraft; hatred, discord, jealousy, fits of rage, selfish ambition, dissensions, factions and envy; drunkenness, orgies, and the like. (Gal. 5:19-21)

Reflect on the list of the acts of the sinful nature. Circle the ones that are present in your church or organization.

Now, think about your own life. Which one(s) from the list above are present?

4. Look at the *Proud People or Broken People* which gives 28 differences between proud and broken people. On each line mark the one that most closely describes your life. After you have finished, take at least 10 minutes in reflective prayer, asking God to shape your life in the areas He is speaking to you about. Then record here any significant insights or new understandings about yourself especially noting how these areas impact your leadership.

PROUD PEOPLE or BROKEN PEOPLE?
Grace4Life © 2006 London UK by John Wade Long, Jr.
Reproduced with permission.

Even a casual glance at Church history will reveal the special spark that has ignited fires of revival in the hearts, homes and churches of God's people: *Gospel brokenness.* Christians are struck afresh with the sense that they are Big Sinners who have a Big Savior. And this brokenness has invariably manifested itself in a certain way—in the personal confession of sin—privately to God, and publicly to others. Indeed, when this spirit of humility has been lacking, the Gospel devolves into an imaginary solution, for the imaginary problem of sin, for imaginary sinners—should there be any present. Take an honest look at your heart and ask yourself,—*"Am I proud, or broken?"*

▽ PROUD PEOPLE...

Psalm 138:6 *Though the LORD is on high, he looks upon the lowly, but the proud he knows from afar.*
1 Peter 5: 5 *Clothe yourselves with humility... for God resists the proud, but gives grace to the humble.*

▽ BROKEN PEOPLE...

Psalm 51:16, 17 *You do not delight in sacrifice, I would bring it... The sacrifices of God are a broken spirit; a broken and contrite heart, O God, you will not despise.*

	Proud People	Broken People
1	**feel** like small sinners; are busy correcting the faults and failures of others	**feel** like big sinners; are busy correcting their own faults and failures
2	**are** self-righteous and have a critical, faultfinding spirit	**are** compassionate and forgiving because they know how much they are forgiven
3	**look** down on others	**esteem** others better than themselves
4	**have** an independent, self-sufficient spirit	**lean** on God and other believers
5	**have** to prove they are right	**realize** that they are often wrong
6	**claim** their rights; have a demanding spirit	**yield** up their rights; have a meek spirit
7	**are** self-protective of their time, their rights, and their reputations	**are** self-sacrificing; give of their time, yield up their rights, and don't need a reputation
8	**want** to be served; but will serve—to earn praise	**want** to serve others for the glory of God
9	**want** success for themselves	**want** to make others successful
10	**are** self-promoting	**want** to see others promoted
11	**want** to be recognized and appreciated; are sad when others receive honors	**have** a sense of their own unworthiness; are surprised when God is able to use

▽ PROUD PEOPLE...

▽ BROKEN PEOPLE...

them

feel that *"This organization/ministry should be thankful they have me."*	12 **know** all they have to offer is God's power blessing others through their weakness
are unteachable; confident they know everything	13 **are** humble and teachable; have much to learn
are self-conscious; are always wondering, *"How do I look?"*	14 **are** self-forgetful; consider others better than themselves
keep others at a distance, are unapproachable and overconfident	15 **risk** letting others get close to them, are tender hearted and vulnerable
are defensive when criticized, feel they're never at fault	16 **are** able to receive criticism with an open, humble spirit
PROUD PEOPLE... are quick to blame others when things go wrong	17 BROKEN PEOPLE... can see when they are wrong and accept responsibility for it
are concerned with looking respectable; must protect their image and reputation	18 **die** to their hunger for reputation and live to promote Christ's reputation
find it difficult to tell others about their spiritual needs (self-protective)	19 **are** willing and able to be open about their spiritual needs (self-disclosing)
cover up their sin; are fearful that someone might find out they're sinful or needy	20 **are** willing to be exposed. Christ is their righteousness; they have nothing to lose.
can't say, "I was wrong"; are evasive and purposely vague when confessing their sins	21 **are** able to acknowledge specific sins and are quick to seek forgiveness - Jas. 5:16
focus on hurts they have received from others; see themselves as victims who need sympathy	22 **focus** on their need for repentance; see themselves as sinners who need a Savior
are concerned about the painful consequences of their sin; are sorry when they get caught — not that they have hurt God and others	23 **are** concerned about their sinful hearts; are grieved that they have hurt God and others; are eager to repent of and forsake their sins
when in conflict, they always wait for the other person to come and say "I'm *sorry.*"	24 **take** the initiative for reconciliation; are the first to say "I am sorry; please forgive me!"
compare themselves with others; are sure they are worthy of special honor	25 **compare** themselves with Jesus; are sure they need God's mercy
are blind to their heart's true condition	26 **see** their Jeremiah 17:9 hearts; walk in the Light
can't think of anything they need to repent of; are self-satisfied	27 **realize** they need a heart attitude of repentance every day of their lives
don't think they need revival—but are quite sure everyone else does	28 **sense** their need for continual revival, cleansing from sin, and the filling of the Holy Spirit

NOTE: We are indebted to Nancy Leigh DeMoss of Campus Crusade for Christ International who presented the essence of this list in an address to their USA National Staff Training Institute in June 1995. Revised for *Grace4Life*.

A Sampler: Spiritual pride & brokenness in the Bible

Isaiah 57:15 For this is what the high and lofty One says—he who lives forever, whose name is holy: "I live in a high and holy place, but also with him who is contrite and lowly in spirit, to revive the spirit of the lowly and to revive the heart of the contrite."

Luke 18:9-14 Jesus' parable to some who were confident of their own righteousness and looked down on everybody else: Two men went up to the temple to pray, one a Pharisee and the other a tax collector. The Pharisee stood up and prayed about himself: "God, I thank you that I am not like other men-robbers, evil-doers, adulterers—or even like this tax collector. I fast twice a week and give a tenth of all I get." But the tax collector stood at a distance. He would not even look up to heaven, but beat his breast and said, "God, have mercy on me, a sinner." I tell you that this man, rather than the other, went home justified before God. *For everyone who exalts himself will be humbled, and he who humbles himself will be exalted."*

Romans 12:1,3,10 Therefore, I urge you, brothers, in view of God's mercy, to offer your bodies as living sacrifices, holy and pleasing to God. This is your spiritual act of worship.' For by the grace given me I say to every one of you: Do not think of yourself more highly than you ought, but rather think of yourself with sober judgment. Be devoted to one another in brotherly love. Honor one another above yourselves.

Philippians 2:1-7 If you have any encouragement from being united with Christ, if any comfort from his love, if any fellowship with the Spirit, if any tenderness and compassion, then make my joy complete by being like-minded, having the same love, being one in spirit and purpose. *Do nothing out of selfish ambition or vain conceit, but in humility consider others better than yourselves.* Each of you should look not only to your own interests, but also to the interests of others. Your attitude should be the same as that of Christ Jesus: Who, being in very nature God, did not consider equality with God something to be grasped, but *made himself of no reputation*, and took the nature of a servant...

BREAKOUT GROUPS:
1. **Mark three items you struggle with on the left side, and if you're willing, share one of them.**
2. **Discuss: If you grew in brokenness, how would that impact your relationship with:**
    a. **God,**
    b. **Your family,**
    c. **Your fellow church members, and**
    d. **Your non-Christian friends?**

Chapter Four

THE LEADER AND MOTIVES

Mark's heart beat rapidly as he sat across the desk from his Bishop. He could not believe his ears. "I want you to go and start a church in the next province," the bishop continued. "If it succeeds, you will be able to support your family well and live like I do." This was the chance he had been waiting for. At last he would be respected and live comfortably.

Pastor Mark worked hard. Day and night he gave himself to his small church. Under his strong leadership the church grew and prospered. People respected him because he worked hard and had a good reputation in the community. When he walked down the road, people always greeted him, "Hello Pastor!" But, after two years of success, a conflict arose between Pastor Mark and his board of elders. The pastor felt that after his years of sacrificial service, the church should pay for him to have a big house and a car. The elders believed he was asking too much. The issue exploded and soon the church was divided.

Although several different things most likely contributed to the trouble, Pastor Mark's motives played a major part in the church division. As the church prospered, Pastor Mark's reasons for leading became less and less desirable, digressing far from God's expectations for his leaders.

This illustration raises a significant question by which all leaders must evaluate themselves. What motivates you to lead? Is it because leadership is fun? Do you seek others' praise and approval? Are you a business leader or educator because of God's call or for personal gain?

This question really addresses your motives. In Christian leadership, your motives are often as crucial as the work you actually do. While many leaders have pure motives, others, like Mark, enter leadership for the wrong reasons. Peter, as an experienced leader, wrote instructions to church leaders that are still relevant today and that will help you examine your own motives for leadership.

> To the elders among you, I appeal as a fellow-elder, a witness of Christ's sufferings and one who also will share in the glory to be revealed. Be shepherds of God's flock that is under your care, serving as overseers – not because you must, but because you are willing, as God wants you to be; not greedy for money, but eager to serve; not lording it over those entrusted to you, but being examples to the flock. And when the Chief Shepherd appears, you will receive the crown of glory that will never fade away (1 Peter 5:1-4).

This passage is full of insight for Christian leaders. In this chapter, I will simply focus on the four motives that Peter highlights for Christian leadership.

The Leader's Motive Is Sincere

Peter, first of all, says that you should enter leadership with a sincere heart. He says that you should serve, not "because you must, but because you are willing, as God wants you to be." Leadership carries heavy responsibility and is not for the unwilling. Christian leadership should never be forced or dictated. Your personal call will often be confirmed by others, but unless it comes from God you will not make it in Christian leadership. Whether in the church, community or society, no Christian leader should hold any position without a clear sense of call from God.

Calling prevents burnout

Without a clear calling, Christian leadership quickly becomes an overwhelming task. Kingdom work is never finished and never will be until Christ's return. You could work and work for years without seeing many results. Often the tangible rewards are few. Many leaders have started the journey but soon faced physical, emotional and/or spiritual exhaustion. They burned out. Without a clear sense of call and a divinely fueled and inspired vision, you will burn out quickly.

Calling provides energy

My call keeps me going. I may be physically worn out, but I remember the call of God upon my life and I keep going. This doesn't mean that I can't stop and rest but my call gives me staying power and motivates me to continue the work, even when it is hard or the fruit is not readily apparent. When I pursue the work that God has called me to, I am energized by God. When the Lord commissions me to do His work, my service becomes both exciting and rewarding.

Calling protects your motives

My call also helps to protect my motives. Sometimes I begin to serve for impure reasons. I may be tempted to serve for money, but then God reminds me that I am called. I may be tempted to please other people, but then God reminds me that He is the one who called me. A clear sense of calling helps to guard my heart against many wrong motives.

Clearly a sense of calling is imperative to pure motives. But how does a leader receive a "call" from God? We cannot explore that issue fully in this chapter, but a few comments are in order. Most people will never have a "Damascus road" call like the apostle Paul experienced. Nevertheless, for some Christian leaders, the "call" of God does come in a supernatural event through which God is speaking. For most, God will probably speak in less dramatic ways.

Some experience God's direction in their life as they develop their gifts and are faithful in serving God where they are. Slowly they are given greater and greater responsibility. Many times the emerging leader does not recognize his own potential but only considers leadership after others begin to affirm his gifts. Through prayer, reflection and counsel, God can confirm that calling.

It is certainly valid for other believers to encourage a person to consider the call of God. Each person must, however, settle the matter fully in his own heart, not based on the opinions of others.

Many church leaders struggle with God over the issue of His call. They sense a call, but it looks overwhelming or too costly. They fear it will lead to a life of poverty for their family. Whenever God calls you to step from the known to the unknown, you will naturally face some fear and questions. Such decisions require prayer, godly counsel and time. The time spent thinking and processing God's call is not wasted. God will purify your motives and instill courage in you so that you will not turn back later. When you have confidence that you are responding to God's call, DO IT. The call may be costly, but it is always less costly than disobedience.

Christian leaders in other spheres likewise should be clearly called to their position or vocation. Career choices should be based on a sense of God's direction, not simply opportunities that are available or financial rewards.

In the final analysis, every Christian leader should be able to say, "I am here because God wants me to be here." Can you say that about your current leadership role?

The Leader's Motive Is To Serve

Peter says that we are "serving as overseers." In modern terms this could read, "Be the boss by serving." This is a paradox, yet it is the

Christian way. In the world, the higher a person rises in leadership, the more people serve him. In the Kingdom, it is just the opposite. Leaders are servants.

Jesus came as a servant. He washed the feet of His disciples and now He calls us to lead as He led. "Even the son of man did not come to be served, but to serve and to give his life as a ransom for many" (Mark 10:45). This applies in the home, on the church

> If you're not ready to serve, get out of Christian leadership!

finance committee, and in the corporate boardroom. As you rise in leadership responsibility, your privileges decrease and your responsibility increases. The higher you rise, the more others demand of you. Your time becomes their time; your resources their resources. Your life becomes an open book.

If you're not ready to serve, get out of Christian leadership. Examine your motives. Do you lead in order to serve or to be served? Realize, also, that the Peter who wrote this passage on leadership is also the same one that argued about being the greatest at the last supper and nearly refused to allow Jesus to wash his feet. God can redeem and transform a man!

Serving also means that you intend to give, rather than receive. Peter cautions you to not be "greedy for money." The desire for money has led many leaders astray inside and outside the church. Even if you receive no monetary rewards in your leadership position, you may still be tempted to serve because of what you will get out of the role. You may earn prestige, a special seat, a title, or public recognition. Having power and authority feels good and many lead because of it.

Serving others requires genuine love. Love looks out for others. Love is generous, eager to see others prosper and grow. How much love do you have for the people you lead?

All leaders are motivated either to get or to give. But according to Peter, Christian leadership is characterized by giving, not receiving. As a leader I am called to give my time, my money, my prayers and my love to serve those under me.

If I am going to give to people, I must receive from somewhere. What is my source? God Himself. This is one of the most awesome benefits of Christian leadership: passing on to others what God has given to you. Leaders must get into the presence of the Lord, receive direction from Him and then pass it on to others. Everyone knows that food tastes better in the kitchen, when it is just coming from the skillet, than when it is served later. If I am a leader whose motive is to serve others and give to them, I will experience this blessing from God. Do you lead to give or to receive, to serve or to be served?

The Leader's Motive Is To Show

Peter tells us to be "examples to the flock" (1 Peter 5:3). Christian leadership focuses on showing rather than telling. You lead others by showing them the way, not just telling them the way. One motive for leadership should be to function as a model for others. You stand as a living demonstration of the power of God to change lives and you can, therefore, call others to imitate you.

Paul says, "Follow me as I follow Christ" (1 Corinthians 11:1). What a powerful challenge. Can I say the same to those who follow me? Do I ever tell others to do what I am not even doing? Telling others what to do is much easier than actually modeling what should be done. But, when you tell your people to be prayerful, you must be prayerful. When you tell them to come to the meeting on time, you must arrive early. This standard brings a real challenge to most leaders. Ask yourself, "If everyone in my organization was like me, what would it be like?"

Leaders can very easily become dictators who tell others what to do without setting an example themselves. Jesus harshly rebuked the Pharisees for just this sort of leadership. The Pharisees led by "lording it over" the people under them. But Peter says, "Not lording it over those entrusted to you." "Lording it over" implies the abuse of authority, the use of position to force obedience, or the use of power for personal benefit.

Lording can be seen when we:
• Refuse to be challenged
• Verbally abuse people
• Demand compensation or privileges
• Manipulate others

Christian leadership does not use force. People are free to follow or not to follow. Your only power is to attract people to you through genuine humility and service. Influence comes through your ability to be a model that others will desire to follow.

As a leader, you can use your position to build yourself up or to build others up. Paul says in 2 Corinthians 13:10, "that when I come I may not have to be harsh in my use of authority — the authority the Lord gave me for building you up, not for tearing you down." People need good, strong leadership. I am not suggesting that you stop exercising good leadership, but that you must exercise it from a position of love and for the benefit of people, not yourself.

If your motive is to model the way, you will need to carefully examine your own life to ensure that you are a worthy example. It is possible to "lord" in places where you have not been faithful yourself, but you can only "lead" by guiding people along a path that you have already traveled. Can others follow your example?

The Leader's Motive Is To Satisfy

Peter's final motive for all Christian leaders is to satisfy the "Chief Shepherd." Peter reminds us in this passage that we are shepherds of God's flock. God is the "Chief Shepherd" (1 Peter 5:4), and is at the top of the administrative chart. The flock is *his flock*, not mine. To be effective in leadership, you need to recognize both God's authority and human authority. You work for Him, under Him and under others. Calling Him "Lord" declares that He has the right to be in total control of your life. Many times, because God is not tangibly sitting in the office next door, spiritual leaders forget that God will hold them accountable, and they begin to act like dictators instead of shepherds. But your motive must be to satisfy your "Boss."

Instead of seeking to satisfy the Lord, you may often be tempted to seek to satisfy others. Your flesh cries out to be liked, to receive applause. But Peter reminds you that you should work, not for the praise of man, but for the praise of your Lord.

Peter also encourages you to look to the future. He talks of the time when the "Chief Shepherd appears." For now He may be hidden from your sight and sometimes you may forget that He is watching your work, but He will appear. Does that promise excite you? Have you been the kind of leader that will be happy to see the Master coming? Some will bow their heads in shame on that day. Others will watch their works be consumed in fire. But those who have served as faithful leaders will receive a "crown of glory" (1 Peter 5:4).

I am excited as I think of the day that Jesus will come and give me a crown. Every believer will receive a reward, but here Peter speaks directly to faithful leaders, to those who have given themselves to the work of the Lord.

This reward is definite. Peter does not say, "You *might*." He says, "You *will*." Worldly leaders receive their rewards on this earth; you will receive your's in heaven. While this life often does hold good rewards for leadership, the more special and eternal rewards will be in heaven. That crown will "never fade away."

Imagine the scene in heaven as God calls Christian leaders, one by one, to receive their reward. What will He say about your leadership? I hope to hear the words, "Here is a leader who served at My call and led with My heart."

This eternal perspective keeps our motives pure. It holds our focus on serving Christ with a pure heart. Take some time and examine your own motives. Why are you a leader? Reflect on the motives Peter gives in this passage and allow God to speak to your heart.

ACTION ASSIGNMENT

1. Take stock of your leadership by honestly answering the following questions based on 1 Peter 5:1-4. Rate yourself from 1-5 on each question, with 5 being "excellent" and 1 being "much improvement needed."

	1	2	3	4	5
1. I have a clear sense of "call" to leadership.					
2. I have the attitude of a servant.					
3. I leading to "give" not to "get."					
4. I am a good example to those that I am serving.					
5. I do not "lord it over" those I am leading.					
6. I am leading to satisfy Christ.					
7. I am submitting to Christ's authority.					
8. I am submitting to the authority of others over me.					
9. I don't use my position for personal advantage.					
10. I have a genuine love for the people under my authority.					

2. After you have evaluated yourself, go back through the questions looking for the areas that you feel God is now calling you to focus on in your development. Put the numbers of two of them here: _2_, _6_

3. Now, write two practical steps you can take to change in the areas you have indicated on the lines above. (This should be an action step, not "trusting God" or "praying" but a clear step you will take.)

   a. actively seeking the meekness & humility of Christ
   b. meditating on what it means to satisfy Jesus

4. Take at least 10 minutes meditating on 1 Peter 5:1-4 allowing God to again speak to you and asking Him to strengthen you in your areas of weakness. Remember, He longs to help you become the leader that He has called you to be! Record any insights below.

Just want to hear Jesus proudly say "well done."

5. Share with your spouse (or close friend if you are not married) what you have learned and the steps you will take. Mark here when you have done this. _____

Chapter Five

THE LEADER AND HIS TONGUE

Imagine that for the last five days you had attached a tape recorder to your body. Every time you spoke, it would record your words. Now on Sunday morning you must play the tape before the whole congregation. Would you enjoy this exercise? Not many people would welcome this kind of exposure.

Your words are powerful. The small tongue inside your mouth is the strongest part of your body. It is so powerful that **Proverbs 18:21** says, **"The tongue has the power of life and death."** With your words you can build or destroy, create friends or enemies. Your words can encourage or discourage; they can speak truth or lies; they can bring peace or tension. Your words can cut like a knife, or heal like a salve. It is with your words that you communicate your deepest feelings, hopes and dreams. You can make someone smile or start a fight; you can create peace or a riot. Your words hold tremendous power.

We can all remember words spoken to us in childhood that still bring a strong sense of joy or pain. Maybe someone told you, "You'll never amount to anything!" To this day you struggle to believe in yourself. Or maybe someone unthinkingly said, "Your nose looks funny," and years later you still wish you could change your nose.

Because you have such a powerful instrument in your mouth, God is very concerned with our speech. The Bible has much to say about our words. The book of Proverbs alone contains over 100 verses (out of 900) that deal with our speech. As a leader, your actions are magnified before others. Your strengths and weaknesses all *look greater than they actually are.* For this reason, it is especially critical that you learn to control your tongue.

Jesus says, "men will have to give account on the Day of Judgment for every *careless* word they have spoken" (Matthew 12:36, italics mine). Jesus reminds us that we will eventually give an account for how we have used our tongues. Jesus will hold us accountable, not only for what we have said in public, but also for our "careless words." Careless words are those that slip out of my mouth before I think. They are the harsh words spoken in anger; the quick retort; the unkind remark; and the exaggeration that boosts my image. This chapter is based on a verse that has changed the way that I talk.

> Do not let any unwholesome talk come out of your mouths, but only what is helpful for building others up according to their needs, that it may benefit those who listen (Ephesians 4:29).

Paul, in this chapter of Ephesians, talks about putting away the old way of life in order to put on the way of Jesus Christ. In this verse he addresses one of the *toughest* areas to change: the way we talk. He gives the standard of Jesus for our tongues.

Jesus Wants Your Tongue To Put Away Unwholesome Talk

Paul first lists what should *not* come out of a believer's mouth: unwholesome talk. The surrounding verses and other scriptures identify some of the unwholesome talk to which Paul referred.

Unwholesome Talk Must Be Identified

Falsehood

A significant area of unwholesome talk is falsehood or lies. Paul says, in Ephesians 4:25, "Therefore each of you must put off falsehood and speak truthfully to his neighbor, for we are all members of one body." Speaking lies can be done **directly** when you openly state something that is not true, "I wasn't there," or "I didn't do it," when in truth you were there and did do it. You can also speak lies by **giving a false impression.** When you say, "I'll be there" and you have no intention of being there, that is a false impression. Sometimes you give a false impression by keeping quiet and allowing others to believe something that you know to be false. Other times you give a false impression with a wonderful testimony: "I'm fine and saved and experiencing victory in the Lord." In reality you may be struggling in a certain area and your assurances are untruthful. Another form of falsehood is **exaggeration.** This "stretching of the truth" makes your story sound much better to your audience. But as soon as you stretch the truth it becomes a lie.

Truthfulness is so crucial for leaders that I have devoted the entire next chapter to look at it more closely.

Words spoken in anger

A second area of unwholesome talk is words spoken in anger. Paul says, "in your anger do not sin" (Ephesians 4:26). This is probably one of the quickest ways to sin with your tongue. **When you are angry, your brain stops functioning properly but your mouth keeps on running.** You may say harsh and cutting words, "I hate you!" or "I'll never work here again!" or "I'll never lend you another book!" You later regret these words but you can never retract them. You can see the hurt in the other person's eyes, but in your anger you feel justified for what you said.

Obscenity

In Ephesians 5:4, Paul says, "Nor should there be obscenity, foolish talk or coarse joking, which are out of place." Obscene language is designed to arouse sexual excitement. It is vulgar, instead of focusing on things that bring glory to God. It is what we sometimes term "off color joking." Avoid jokes or stories that focus on sexual activities or on the anatomy of the body. The jokes may be humorous, but they are designed to arouse us in ways that are not pleasing to God. They devalue your brothers and sisters in Christ and degrade your physical body and the act of sex, instead of honoring God's creation.

Foolish talk

In the same verse Paul warns against "foolish talk." So much of the world's talk is completely foolish. You can listen for 20 minutes and at the end you say, "So what?" It lacks any value or meaning. It may not be bad, but it is not good either. This does not mean that a believer cannot engage in casual conversation, but this should only occupy a small fraction of your talk and it should always lead to more meaningful conversation. In 2 Timothy 2:23, Paul warns Timothy, a leader, "Don't have anything to do with foolish and stupid arguments, because you know they produce quarrels."

Coarse joking

Paul also speaks in the same verse against "coarse joking." Paul does not condemn all jokes, but he specifically mentions "coarse" jokes. Joking and laughter are essential to a joyful Christian life. In fact, many Christian leaders desperately need to learn to enjoy life and have a good laugh. A leader who enjoys a good joke, even one at his own expense, is refreshing. But while jokes are good, you must carefully guard the kind of things that make you laugh. Jokes that mock another person or culture or that dishonor God's creation should be avoided. If you have doubts, the joke probably is not worth laughing at or repeating to others.

Too many words

Sometimes unwholesome talk is manifested simply through talking too much. We all know people who always have something to say, who will say everything they know and then continue to talk, who have a comment on every issue and an opinion for every topic.

But talking too much has some serious consequences. Proverbs 10:19, says, "When words are many, sin is not absent." Those who talk too much will inevitably end up sinning with their speech.

> Those who talk too much will inevitably end up committing another sin with their speech.

When the truth has been exhausted, lies will follow. When a good report is over, a bad report will unfold. When kind words are used up, slander and gossip will begin. When healthy jokes are finished, bad ones will follow. 2 Timothy 2: 16, written to a leader, says, "Avoid godless chatter because those who indulge in it will become more and more ungodly."

Those who talk too much also sin because they fail to listen to others. James 1:19 says, "Everyone should be quick to listen, slow to speak, and slow to become angry." God gave people two ears and one mouth. Consider that a divine mandate to listen twice as much as you talk! Remember that you will win more friends with your ears than with your mouth.

The writer of Ecclesiastes (5:1-3) even warns us not to talk to God too much. Keep your prayers free of unnecessary words. I wonder how often God gets tired of listening to me, and wishes that I would just listen.

Beware of the person who talks too much. He has a problem.

Flattery

Flattery is saying nice things about people in order to win their favor. Proverbs 26:28 warns that "a flattering mouth works ruin." People who use flattery think they can control others with their tongues. You may not call it flattery, but "buttering up" or other nicer sounding words. "Pastor, that was a dynamic sermon, I was so blessed.... could you help me with a problem?" God's kingdom holds no place for manipulative words of flattery. Give honest compliments instead.

Swearing

Another area of unwholesome talk for the believer is swearing. In Matthew 5, Jesus clearly commands His followers not to swear:

> But I tell you, do not swear at all: either by heaven, for it is God's throne; or by the earth, for it is His footstool; or by Jerusalem, for it is the city of the Great King. And do not swear by your head, for you cannot make even one hair white or black. Simply let your "Yes" be "Yes", and your "No", "No"; anything beyond this comes from the evil one (Matthew 5:34-37).

I believe Jesus commands us not to swear because the need to swear indicates that a person does not always tell the truth. If I say, "I swear that I'm telling the truth" I am implying that you should believe me now but not every other time. Jesus said, therefore, "Let your 'yes' be 'yes' and your 'no', 'no.'" Very simply, He commands us to tell the truth all the time.

Swearing is closely related to using God's name in vain. Many believers use God's name very casually in conversation or as an exclamation. Be careful to honor God's name by using it respectfully.

Gossiping (Proverbs 16:28; 18:8, I Timothy 5:13)

Gossip is saying things about a person that shouldn't be said. Gossip is truly one of the most damaging sins in the church and in the marketplace. Proverbs 16:28 says that "a gossip separates close friends." Many, many relationships have been destroyed by gossip. So often close friends become enemies after gossip creates misunderstanding and distrust. Not only has it ruined individual relationships, gossip has split churches and destroyed organizations. It is a deadly sin.

You may think that you just have to tell someone what you heard or something about a certain person. The information seems to burn within you. *But you do not need to repeat everything that you know.* It is possible to keep quiet.

The most deadly form of gossip is when Christians disguise it with a thin covering of spirituality. This "spiritual gossip" often starts as a prayer request. "Oh, brother, we need to pray for Jane, did you hear what she did the other day..." Don't be deceived. This conversation probably will not end in prayer for Jane. It is **gossip**.

In your flesh, you desire to know everything about other people. We all do. Gossip feels good and it meets this desire. **Proverbs 18:8** says, "The words of a gossip are like choice morsels: they go down to a man's inmost parts." You also feel important when you are able to pass on information that others do not know. You feel superior to the person you are reporting on because you have not sinned like they have. Do not be deceived. Gossip always tears people down; it never builds up.

Slander

Slander is saying something untrue about a person, deliberately spreading a false report. Slander differs from gossip, in that gossip is often true, but should not be shared, while slander is always false and is intended to harm.

We can slander others without realizing it if we fail to check the facts before passing information to someone else. *Beware of passing along second-hand information for which you have no factual verification.* Of course, if you avoid spreading negative information in general, you will be safe from both gossip and slander. Proverbs 10:18 says, "Whoever spreads slander is a fool." In Titus 3:1-2 we are reminded to "slander no one." Slander is a deadly sin and it has destroyed many Christian leaders.

Your mouth can speak unwholesome words in many other ways that this limited space will not allow us to examine in depth. These include: grumbling, quarreling, complaining, boasting, criticizing and filthy language, among others.

Unwholesome Talk Must Be Stopped

Not only should you identify your unwholesome talk, you need to stop it. Paul commands, "Do not let any unwholesome talk come out of your mouths" (Ephesians 4:29). He does not offer this as a suggestion for those who want to be first class believers or as a prayer request. Paul *commands* you to speak in a wholesome manner.

You control your tongue and you must accept responsibility for your words. Do not say, "He made me say that!" The truth is, you say only what you chose to say. Do not shift responsibility to your mother: "Well my mother was always a big talker." Others may influence you in significant ways, but they do not make you gossip. Only when you stop thinking as a victim and accept responsibility, will God be able to change and redeem your words.

Paul challenges you to completely eliminate unwholesome talk. *Do not allow **any** unwholesome talk to come out of your mouth.* Reducing the amount or degree of unwholesome talk in our lives is desirable, but it is not sufficient. Paul does not want to reduce the flow of garbage; he **wants to eliminate it all together.**

Even if you obeyed only this part of the verse, your speech would immediately improve at least 50 percent and the number of words you speak would also probably be reduced by more than 50 percent.

Having looked at what you are to eliminate from your tongue, let us look at Jesus' purpose for your tongue. Jesus desires to eliminate the bad, yes, but He also wants to redeem your speech for His glory.

Jesus Wants Your Tongue To Build Others Up

Paul says that your tongue should speak "only what is helpful for building others up according to their needs, that it may benefit those who listen." God intends your words primarily for building others up or edification. In this passage, Paul gives several characteristics of edifying talk.

Edifying talk meets the needs of others

Paul says that your speech should be according to "their needs," in order to bless and edify others. Stop and analyze your speech. Much speech focuses on meeting personal needs, rather than the needs of our listeners:

- You may have a need to be *recognized*, so you tell funny jokes or talk loudly so that others will notice you.
- You may have a need to feel *important*, so you discuss the weakness of another person, in order to elevate yourself to a superior position.
- You may have a need to be *loved*, so you speak words of flattery, hoping to win attention and approval from others.
- You may have a need to feel *accepted*, so you share only what you think others want to hear.

is this why I joke in certain ways?

If you are like most people, many of your words focus on your own needs, not the needs of the other person. As a believer, that focus must shift. As you model the sort of love that God has towards you, an unselfish, giving love, you will focus on the needs of others:

- They need to be *recognized*. Listen intently and validate their contributions.

- They need to feel *important*. Compliment the strengths that you observe and encourage them to walk in those abilities more fully.
- They need to feel *loved*. Tell them, "I love you" and show it by your actions.
- They need to feel *accepted*. Tell them about your own struggles so that they can share theirs without feeling alone.

Your words should reach out, like the comfort of God, and meet the needs of those around you. Before you open your mouth, ask yourself, "What does this person need and how can I bless him with my words?"

Edifying talk benefits the listener

Paul exhorts us to speak so that our words "may benefit those who listen." When you speak according to the needs of others, your words will have the power to bring blessing and healing.

You may know a person who always seems to speak helpful and encouraging words to you. When you are having a bad day, you want to visit her because you know that her words will be a salve. I love to be around people like that. I have a friend who always has a positive word for me and I make a point of seeing him often. Such people are rare jewels. As a Christian and leader, seek to become a person like that.

After every conversation you should be able to say, "I ministered to that person." This does not mean that you always say what people want to hear or that you cannot deliver a rebuke or challenge. Sometimes a rebuke is exactly what they need. But rebukes must come in love, to help meet the need they have. So in every case, whether in encouragement, challenge or rebuke, let your conversation bring benefit to the other person.

Edifying talk is the exclusive talk of the believer

Paul says that "*only* what is helpful for building others up" should come out of your mouth. Your mouth should specialize in this kind of talk and speak nothing else. Obedience to this command will eliminate unwholesome and unnecessary talk. Imagine the revolutionary impact that this could have in your family and in your church.

Jesus Wants Your Tongue To Be Changed

By this time you may be discouraged. You may feel like your tongue is out of control and change seems impossible. Here are four steps that can help you change your tongue.

Confess your sin

Christ can only change you if you first acknowledge your sin. "If we confess our sins, He is faithful and just and will forgive us our sins and purify us from all unrighteousness" (1 John 1:9). His promise depends on your willingness to repent. You must acknowledge your words as sin, instead of justifying yourself by calling them a weakness or a problem. And when you confess your sin, be specific. The Lord is not impressed with your generalities. You must humble yourself enough to say, "My tongue is full of gossip," "I lied to my boss," or "I slandered my friend."

Confess your sin to God and, when necessary, to others. If you have sinned with your tongue, undoubtedly you have offended someone. Confession is one of the most powerful incentives toward change. Going to the person you have wronged and asking for forgiveness is very painful, but it will help you to take the issue seriously. You will think twice before repeating that sin because you remember the pain of confession. Do not take shortcuts to build your character. Pay the price and God will change your tongue. I remember many painful times when I had to ask someone's forgiveness for speaking harshly or wrongly. It has changed me and it will change you.

Ask God to change your heart

If you have a problem with your tongue, you may ask God to change your speech. But the root of the problem is not your tongue, but your heart. Luke 6:45 says, "For out of the overflow of the heart the mouth speaks." Your tongue problems are really heart problems. You hurt others with your harsh words because your heart is not broken; you gossip because you have pride and want to look good; you lie because you want others to think well of you; and you slander because you hate another person. Think about how you struggle with words, and ask the Lord to identify the root issue in your heart. Then ask God to change your heart.

Memorize the Word

The best way to change your heart is to get the Word of God deep into your heart and mind through memorization. David says, "How can a young man keep his way pure? By living according to your word… Your word I have hid in my heart that I might not sin against you" (Psalm 119:9,11). Memorize scripture and the power of God's Word will begin to purify your speech. Especially memorize verses that deal with the problems you have. Begin with our key verse in Ephesians 4:29. If your problem is lying, memorize verses that speak of lying. If it is gossip, memorize verses that deal with that subject. The Word of God will begin to change your tongue.

Give God time

Change takes time. Don't expect your speech to change completely overnight. You probably learned your current speech habits over the course of a lifetime and it will take time to change them.

God does want to totally transform your tongue as you allow Him to work in your life. Philippians 1:6 says, "He who began a good work in you will carry it on to completion until the day of Christ Jesus." Let Him begin that good work on your tongue today.

As a young man, I had a very sharp and witty tongue. My friends and I would continually wage war with our words, seeing who could outdo the other. Someone would tell me, "Jon, you can't sing at all!" I would reply, "Yeah, but you are so bad that when you sing all the birds fly away!" Back and forth we would "joke," laughing all the time, but inwardly crying as we wounded each other's fragile self-esteem. After some time God began to deal with my heart and I realized that He did not want me to speak this way with others. I repented and began the long road to victory in this area. It took a long time for me to break those habits but slowly I learned to use my tongue to build others up instead of tearing them down.

My prayer is that today you will begin the same process in your life. You may need God's help in a different area than I did, but His power to change you stays the same. As I write these words, I am praying for you that, when you read this, God will speak to your heart and begin to change your tongue. Take some time with Him now and reflect on how you have used your tongue. Go ahead, put the book down. God is ready to meet with you now.

ACTION ASSIGNMENT

1. Evaluate your tongue in each of the following areas. Mark the column that best describes your tongue from one to five (one is very bad; five is totally Spirit-controlled.)

Area of speech evaluated	1	2	3	4	5	Comment
1. Lying				/		I don't lie out of habit sub m
2. Words spoken in anger			/			
3. Obscenity			/			
4. Foolish talk		/				
5. Coarse joking				/		
6. Too many words		/				
7. Flattery				/		
8. Swearing			/			
9. Gossiping				/		
10. Slander					/	

2. Now go to a very close friend (your spouse if you are married.) Ask them to do the same evaluation about your speech. Do not allow them to see the one you did above. Ask them to be totally honest. Remember, "Wounds from a friend can be trusted." (Proverbs 27:6)

Area of speech evaluated	1	2	3	4	5	Comment
1. Lying						
2. Words spoken in anger						
3. Obscenity						
4. Foolish talk						
5. Coarse joking						
6. Too many words						
7. Flattery						
8. Swearing						
9. Gossiping						
10. Slander						

3. After comparing both your evaluation and that of your friend, which are the two areas that need the most improvement in your life? _____and _____. Ask your spouse (or the person who evaluated you) to pray with you, asking God for change in those areas. Put an "x" here when you have done this _____.

4. Think about the two areas that you mentioned above that need improvement in your life. What are the "needs" that you have which contribute to that manner of speaking? _____

_____

_____

    What "heart" problem might it be related to? (pride, selfishness, envy, lust, etc.) _____ Ask God to change your heart in this area.

5. Memorize Eph. 4:29 in a translation of your choice. After you have memorized it find someone to listen to you say it.

Chapter Six

THE LEADER AND TRUTHFULNESS

When is the last time you heard a lie? Most likely you have heard one today, unless you are reading this early in the morning. I won't ask you when the last time is you *told* a lie. Lies are more a part of our lives and our culture than we would like to admit. A survey of modern-day morality in Britain recently reported that the average person lies 20 times a day.[17] Truthfulness significantly affects our character and our capacity to lead.

The Expectation Of Truthfulness

The Bible clearly expects us to be truthful. Here are just a few of the clear biblical teachings concerning truthfulness and lying:

---

[17]Gerry Loughran, "Being ecomomical with the truth now in vogue," *Sunday Nation*, Februrary 2002 [newspaper on-line]; available from http://www.nationaudio.com/News/DailyNation/24022002/Comment/LetterLondon38.html; Internet.

"Do not steal. Do not lie. Do not deceive one another" (Leviticus 19:11).

"The LORD detests lying lips, but he delights in men who are truthful" (Proverbs 12:22).

"Truthful lips endure forever, but a lying tongue lasts only a moment" (Proverbs 12:19).

"Therefore each of you must put off falsehood and speak truthfully to his neighbor, for we are all members of one body" (Ephesians 4:25).

"But the cowardly, the unbelieving, the vile, the murderers, the sexually immoral, those who practice magic arts, the idolaters and *all liars*—their place will be in the fiery lake of burning sulfur. This is the second death" (Revelation 21:8, emphasis mine).

"Simply let your 'yes,' be 'yes' and your 'no,' 'no' (Matthew 5:37).

Biblical Principles Of Truthfulness

In addition to the clear commands of Scripture, I find two biblical principles that relate to lying.

Deception can be a generational sin

If not dealt with, the sin of lying will be passed on to the next generation. Abraham told a half lie about his wife, Sarah (Genesis 20:1,12). His son Isaac repeated the same lie (Genesis 26:7). Isaac's son Jacob deceived him in order to steal his brother's birthright and was known as a schemer (Genesis 27). In turn Jacob's sons convinced their father that a wild animal had killed Joseph (Genesis 37).

If you grew up in a family of deceivers, you will struggle more with this sin. When deceit becomes a generational sin, it is rooted deeply in your life and only the power of God can set you free. Lying may be so habitual that you may not even recognize your own lies. The good news is that if you deal with deceit in your own life, you will lay a good foundation for your children and the generations to follow.

Truth and love are not incompatible

You may often feel caught between speaking the truth and loving someone. Many times people lie because they think it will save relationships. They value love over truth. But the Bible teaches that truth and love must work together. Paul says in Ephesians 4:15, "Instead, speaking the *truth in love*, we will in all things grow up into him who is the Head, that is, Christ." You do not need to choose *between* the two, you choose *truth in love*. Suppose that my wife makes a meal and forgets the salt. I can say, "This food tastes awful!" When she looks offended, I reply, "But it's the truth, and the truth will set you free!" Yes, I spoke the truth, but without love. If I learn to balance truth and love I might say, "My dear, thanks for all the work you did to prepare this meal for us. A little more salt would make it a feast fit for a king!"

The Difficulty Of Truthfulness

Let's face it, lying is often much easier than telling the truth. Lying is deeply ingrained in our sinful nature. Children do not have to be taught to lie; they instinctively do it when they realize that it may be to their advantage. Let's think first about *why* we lie and then examine *how* we lie.

Why We Lie

People lie for many different reasons, but most of them fall under a few general categories.

Lying seems like an easy solution to your dilemma

We often lie in difficult situations. You may have done wrong or failed to do what you were supposed to do. You feel cornered. Lying provides a painless escape from the problem. Suppose you overslept and arrive at work late. The boss is not happy. He asks, "Why are you late?" You have two alternatives. You can speak the truth and face the painful consequences or you can lie and hopefully avoid the consequences.

The lie is attractive because it seems to offer a way of escape. Quickly you find yourself saying, "My car had a flat tire and delayed me." The boss is satisfied and you breathe a sigh of relief. It works until your coworker offers to take you to get the tire repaired. Then you need another lie to cover up the first one. Soon you are caught in a cycle of lying and carry around the burden of deceit everywhere you go.

Lying can cause people to think well of you

Often when we lie it is so that others will think more highly of us. You may fear that acknowledging the truth about who you are or what you have done will make you seem less of a leader. Because you are not grounded in God's grace, you crave human affirmation. You want to appear holy before people because you believe that if people really knew you, they would stop loving you. So you resort to lies, exaggerating the story to make yourself look better, or saying, "I've been praying for you," when you have not prayed. You want to maintain a good image.

But, when you lie to gain approval, you simply demonstrate your own sense of inferiority. You need to accept God's grace and not worry about what others think. And you will find that your honesty will lead others to share honestly, and will allow for deeper relationships based upon grace instead of performance.

Lying saves you from confrontation

Sometimes you may lie to avoid confronting a person or an issue. You might fear telling someone that his performance is not satisfactory, so you tell him it is "OK." You might fear an argument, so you pretend that the issue does not matter to you. Someone may do things that really annoy you, but you smile and greet them as though everything is normal. In these situations *we value relationships over truth*. But remember that we are to "speak the truth in love." This delicate balance between truth-telling and compassion maintains the integrity of the relationship and the truth. You can, with God's help, do both. Often the greatest expression of love you can show someone is to tell them the truth.

Lying is natural

You also lie simply because it springs naturally from your sinful nature. You do not need to teach your children to lie; it comes naturally. No one needs a class on "The Art of Lying." We inherited a sinful nature from our parents and ultimately from the devil. As for Satan, lying is his mother tongue! Jesus said:

> You belong to your father, the devil, and you want to carry out your father's desire. He was a murderer from the beginning, not holding to the truth, for there is no truth in him. When he lies, he speaks his *native* language, for he is a liar and the father of lies (John 8:44, italics mine).

Your native language is very easy for you to speak. Words flow out naturally, without thought about meaning or sentence construction. In the same way, when the devil speaks, he does not think about lies, they just effortlessly flow out of his mouth. He spoke the first recorded lie in human history, when he told Eve, "You will not surely die" (Genesis 3:4). When Eve believed his lie, Satan's native language became, apart from Christ's grace, the native language of the human race.

The nature of God, on the other hand, is **truth**. In fact, Scripture says that it is impossible for God to lie. Numbers 23:19 states, "God is not a man, that He should lie, nor a son of man, that He should change His mind. Does He speak and then not act? Does He promise and not fulfill?" The writer of Hebrews 6:18 confirms this fact when he says, "God did this so that, by two unchangeable things in which *it* *is impossible for God to lie,* we who have fled to take hold of the hope offered to us may be greatly encouraged" (italics mine).

God *is* truth. He says, "I am the way and the truth and the life" (John 14:6). Truth is part of His identity and He has nothing to do with things that are hidden, twisted or exaggerated. His Word is more binding than any earthly contract. His "I will do it" means simply that. He is a God of truth and we are called to reflect His character. When we lie, we reflect the nature of the devil instead.

Lying is encouraged by your culture

Not only does the human nature tend towards lies, but your culture also expects and encourages lying. Cultures differ in their expressions of this sin, but all cultures manifest dishonesty in some form. Some cultures expect lying from politicians. Some excuse dishonesty for doctors who don't want to make their patient anxious with bad news. Many cultures teach that it is acceptable to lie in response to the question, "How do you like my dress?" Others expect craftsmen to regularly lie in order to gain their customers' business.

Take a moment and reflect on how your culture encourages lies and ask God for His grace to help you break free from this bondage.

How We Lie

Let's look more closely at the ways in which we lie, in order to help us identify the ways in which we may be speaking dishonestly without realizing it.

Directly

A **direct** lie openly contradicts the truth. You may say, "I wasn't there" or "I didn't do it," when in reality you were there and did do it. This is what we most commonly think of when discussing lying, probably because it is the easiest kind of lie to identify and the most obvious contradiction of the truth.

Exaggeration

Exaggeration is otherwise known as "stretching the truth" or "adding salt" in order to make the story sound better. The temptation to exaggerate often creeps into my life when I have tried to contact someone by phone, perhaps twice. When I finally reach the person I'm tempted to say, "I've been trying all day to get you!" True? No, but I want him to think better of me, so I exaggerate the truth. Concern for my image always motivates exaggeration.

Evangelistic exaggeration often tempts leaders in the church. For example, you lead a crusade and 13 people get saved. Later, someone asks you about the mission and you say, "Around 15 people got saved." Why not, "Around 10?" Because 15 makes you look better! Business leaders are continually tempted to find ways to make the figures look better than reality. Can the truth really be stretched or exaggerated? Certainly not! Truth is inflexible and as soon as we "stretch" it, we speak a lie.

"Children" lies

Another way that we lie involves our children. We often speak untruths, in various forms, to our children. As a parent, you may tell **fairy tales** or stories about life origins that are not true. Your child asks, "Where did I come from?" and you reply, "We got you at the market," or, "We got you at the hospital." As the child grows, she will discover that babies do not come from the market and that her parents lied to her. This does not mean that fables are off-limits, but that they should always be explained as fictional.

Another form of parental dishonesty is the **threat of punishments** that you never intend to fulfil. "If you do that again I'm going to throw you into the fire!" or "If you don't behave, the big, ugly monster will come get you." "Stop crying and I'll bring you a sweet when I get back." This manipulation will only teach your children not to trust you.

You may also **use your children to lie for you**. For example, if an unwanted visitor comes to the door, you might tell your child to,

"Tell him I'm not here." You will be rightly repaid for teaching your child dishonesty if he goes to the door and says, "Daddy says that he's not at home!"

In another scenario, you might send your child to the shop with instructions to tell the owner that you haven't yet received your salary and, therefore, cannot pay him. But your child knows that you have received it, and silently learns your methods of lying.

As your children grow up, they will eventually realize that you have spoken many lies to them. Not only will this experience teach them that lying is permissible and desirable in some cases, but it will also perpetuate a generational cycle of lies. Your children will repeat those same lies to their children, who will repeat them to their children, and so forth. Each generation will reap the fruit of dishonesty from their parents.

The final and most significant way that you might lie to your children is about their **identity**. "You're a stupid boy!" "You'll never succeed in life." "You can't do anything right." "You're a useless person." "You're as stupid as your dad." Not only are they lies, but these words also cut directly to a child's heart and do tremendous damage to his self-image. Your children will become what you say, so speak the true blessings of Christ rather than curses.

False impressions

We lie also when we **give a false impression.** When you say, "I'll be there" and you have no intention of being there, you have given someone a false impression. "I'll pay you back tomorrow" is often an empty promise. Sometimes you give false impressions simply by keeping quiet and allowing others to believe something that you know to be false.

Sometimes a **testimony** gives a false impression. "I'm fine and saved and experiencing victory in the Lord." In reality you may be struggling and your blanket assurances are dishonest. This does not mean that you need to reveal all of your struggles to every person you know, but it does mean that you should not deliberately give others the wrong impression.

You can also give false impressions by **allowing wrong assumptions**. Joseph's brothers did this in Genesis 37:32. "They took the ornamented robe back to their father and said, 'We found this. Examine it to see whether it is your son's robe.'" They did not lie directly, but they led their father to believe that his son had been killed in an accident when they knew very well that this had not happened.

Telling only part of a story can be deceitful. Often you may tell only the parts that make you look good. For that reason, if you tell a story and later find that it isn't true, or that you had missed a significant part, you must go back and correct your story.

Acts 23:27 gives a very intriguing example of slanting the truth to your advantage. The Romans arrested Paul and nearly beat him before they discovered that he was a Roman citizen. Later, when the commander needed to send Paul to another place, he said, "This man was seized by the Jews and they were about to kill him, but I came with my troops and rescued him, for *I had learned that he is a Roman citizen*" (italics mine). True, the commander had learned Paul was a Roman citizen, but through a slight twist in his wording, he gave the impression that he came to Paul's rescue *because* he was a Roman citizen. The facts, as recorded in chapter 22, show that the commander only discovered that Paul was a Roman citizen *after* he had ordered him flogged. But that truth was not to the commander's advantage, so he gave a false impression.

Another biblical example of giving the wrong impression comes from the life of Abraham. Genesis 20:2 records, "and there Abraham said of his wife Sarah, 'She is my sister.' Then Abimelech, king of Gerar, sent for Sarah and took her." What he said was, in a sense, true as Sarah was related to him (see Genesis 20:12). Still, his intent was to deceive.

Keeping quiet

One of the simplest ways to lie in some situations is to keep quiet. This is usually a way of giving a false impression, but it needs special mention here since it is so subtle.

Keeping quiet happens actively in a situation where someone asks, "Does anyone here know about brother Jim?" You know, but you keep quiet, giving the impression that you don't know anything.

You can also keep silent passively, when you see the problems in a situation, but you choose to keep quiet rather than taking the proper steps to report or confront the issue. Of course, knowing the right thing to do and the proper time to do it requires wisdom, but we should never fear speaking the truth.

Another way that silence can be dishonest surfaces during a meeting in which everyone is asked for his or her opinion before passing a resolution or decision. You keep quiet, giving the impression that you agree, until after the meeting when you grumble about the decision to all your friends. Not only is this lying, it is also disloyalty.

To earn money

Sometimes Christians lie in order to make money. The Bible says in Proverbs 21:6, "A fortune made by a lying tongue is a fleeting vapor and a deadly snare." Lying can make a fortune. Many businesses have based their success on regular lies to the customers, creditors, bank, suppliers, etc.

It's very easy to say, "This is good quality" when you know that it is not the best, or, "I just got this vegetable fresh from the farmer this morning," when all you really did was throw fresh water on it this morning. Another common business lie is, "I'll have it finished for you by Tuesday," when you know that you cannot do it until at least Thursday. The craftsman knows that if he tells you the truth you might go elsewhere, so he tells you a lie in order to keep your business. Business is so profit-oriented that lying can become very tempting to use any means, including lies, to gain more money.

People often lie to get jobs. They may cheat on certificates, speak of experience that they do not have or commit to something they cannot follow through with, just to get the job. They may lie about their marital status or place of birth or any other details that might increase their chances of getting the job.

We can see that lying requires only a little bit of creativity! More sobering is the reality that we all lie more than we like to confess. This section is written to heighten your awareness of the many forms dishonesty takes. Now let's examine more closely what truthfulness looks like.

The "LOOK" Of Truthfulness

What will truthfulness look like in different areas of your life?

In your home

At home you tend to let down your guard and relax. Often this means that more of your sinful nature leaks out and that your truthfulness will be severely tested in your families. If you want to succeed as an honest leader, you must first learn to be truthful in your homes.

> One of the greatest gifts that you can give to your family is a truthful tongue.

If you are committed to truth at home **you will speak words of truth** to your children. You will provide positive verbal affirmation that builds and strengthens your children's self image and confidence. You have tremendous power to shape their futures by the words you speak to them in the present. You can choose to affirm their good behavior instead of quickly pointing out mistakes. Positive affirmation will not spoil a child. You should also speak to them about your love. All parents love their children but few speak it. Every child longs to hear a parent say, "I love you."

If you are serious about truthfulness at home, you **will discipline your children when you find them lying.** Too often lying is seen as a "cute" reflection of adult behavior and not the ugly reflection of the devil that it really is. It is never too early to discipline children for lying. As with all discipline, it should be done in love and with kindness, but be sure to deal with lying at an early age. Through your words and actions, make sure that your child knows how seriously you value truthfulness.

Truthfulness will also enable you to be **honest and open with your spouse.** You will make an effort to "unveil" yourself and share deeply. You will not try to find excuses for your behavior but take responsibility when you act wrongly. You will not try to hide money, but will report accurately what you have done with the money you have spent. A wife will no longer say, "I bought food," when she actually bought a new dress. A husband will reveal his true salary and talk openly together about how to budget the money.

One of the greatest gifts that you can give to your family is a truthful tongue.

In your work

Your commitment to truth will also be tested in your workplace. Being truthful means providing totally correct information for your bosses. It means refusing to "slant" reports to your advantage. As honest employees, you will give the true reasons for your lateness or your need for time off. You will honestly report your income for tax purposes. You will give factual information about your products. You will not give a false impression of activity by hanging your coat on the chair and then leaving for the day. You will accurately report reimbursable expenses. You will not take items belonging to your employer for personal use.

In your business, speak the truth even if you risk losing business. Strive to keep all promises you make to a customer. Do not exaggerate your actual costs in order to increase the selling price. Sell your product at prices that are honest and fair both to the customer and to your own business. Do not try to avoid paying taxes on your income, even if it is easy to falsify the records. Use honest weights and measures as you deal with customers.

In leadership

Leaders are held to a higher standard in all areas and truthfulness is no exception. The words that the leader speaks make a significant impact on the lives of the listeners. Leaders must carefully communicate truth in a positive way if they want to be effective. This is the subtle balance of "truth in love" that I have already noted.

Following are three **leadership "truth declarations"** that can guide us as leaders in speaking the truth to the people we lead.

1. I will always give accurate information to my people

You will use wisdom to know what needs to be shared with others, but it must *always* be true. If God expects you to speak truth privately, He also expects your public words to be reliable. You will not give misleading excuses in announcements: "Due to unavoidable circumstances, we have cancelled the meeting." If you failed to plan, admit it! The people who listen to you should be able to know with confidence that everything you say is completely true.

2. I will not withhold information from people unnecessarily

Leaders often withhold information from their people, shrouding leadership in a mysterious cloak that excludes all except the top leaders. You say, "The people can't handle this" or, "They're not mature enough." How mature does someone need to be for the truth? Of course, when leaders are discussing a case of sin or a sensitive business issue, they need to be careful about how much information they make public and when. But many issues leaders deal with are not sensitive and can be shared openly with people. Let them know what you are doing and ask for their support. When too much information is withheld, people begin to lose trust in the leader. The climate of secrecy then breeds gossip and rumors. Often the rumors that result are more damaging than the truth. Many times you wrongly assume that people are totally ignorant of a particular situation, when in reality they often know or at least partially sense, what is happening. Perhaps at the root of this problem is pride in the leader's heart. Be careful that you do not withhold information in order to increase your own sense of self-importance.

3. I will take the blame instead of passing it on to others

This does not mean that you do not announce other's mistakes, but it does mean that as much as possible you must admit your own failures, especially when they affect those under you. When you fail as a leader there is no reason, other than pride, to not admit the truth and ask for forgiveness. This is hard and requires brokenness in spirit, but it is vital if you want to reap the rewards of truthfulness.

The Reward Of Truthfulness

Truthfulness looks like a big job, but it is worth the effort. Not only does it make you more like Christ, but it also brings to you something that is indispensable for leadership: **trust**. ***Trust is the reward of truthfulness.*** When you are consistently truthful, you earn trust from your people. You cannot buy trust; you can only earn it.

Without trust a leader cannot lead. People will not continue to willingly follow a leader that they cannot trust. Maxwell says, "Followers do not trust leaders whose character they know to be flawed, and they will not continue following them."[18] It is only a matter of time before people walk away from a leader they cannot trust.

Trust is a character issue and a matter of becoming more like Christ. Christ not only spoke the truth but he claimed "I am…the truth" (John 14:6). As a leader, when you reflect the truthful character of Christ, followers will learn to trust you.

Your followers will use your truthfulness as a measurement of your

---

[18] Maxwell, *The 21 Indispensable Qualities of a Leader*, 5.

character. A flaw in your character will lessen your ability to lead. You cannot continually deceive people and expect them to trust you. Work on your character. **Become a more trustworthy person and you will be a better leader.** Ask yourself, "Do my people see me as a truthful person? Do my children know me as one who *always* speaks the truth?"

The Road To Truthfulness

How do you become a person of truth? There are several steps you can take to become truthful. They are not easy, but they will work. Because truth is often a matter of how you speak, the steps are similar to those used in the section on gaining control of your speech.

Commit to being a truthful person (Matthew 5:37)
The first step deals with your desire. You must decide to become a truthful person, not only speak truthfully, but also to live a life of truth. This means a continual striving toward greater honesty and integrity, with the awareness that it will take time and effort to break the long chains that lies have wrapped around your heart. It will be painful. But when you make the commitment that whatever it takes, however long it takes, **you want to be a person of truth,** God will begin to change you. Your goal is to obey Jesus' words, "Let your 'Yes' be 'Yes' and your 'No,' 'No' " (Matthew 5:37).

Confess your sin (1 John 1:9)
Second, you must acknowledge that your lying is sin. It is not a weakness or a problem, but a sin. God's solution for sin is confession. He waits to act until you acknowledge your sin and humble yourself before Him.

You must confess your sin to God and, when necessary, to others. Often when you have wronged someone by lying, the most helpful step toward change is to go to that person and ask forgiveness. That is painful, but it will help you to take the issue seriously and will cause you to reconsider the next time that you are tempted to lie. Make a list of the people you have lied to and beginning with the most difficult one, go and ask their forgiveness.

Ask God to change your heart (Luke 6:45)
When you have a problem with truth, the root of the problem is your heart. Luke 6:45 says, "For out of the overflow of the heart the mouth speaks." You lie because you are *afraid* to open yourself to others. You lie because you *want to look good.* You lie because *you don't love enough* to confront. **When you have a truth problem, check your heart.** You need to ask God to do heart surgery on you, giving you His soft, loving heart. Only then will your speech be totally honest. When Christ deals with the root sin in your heart, the fruit (lying) will soon disappear.

> When you have a truth problem you need to check your heart.

Memorize the Word (Psalm 119:9,11)
The best way to change your heart is to get the Word of God deep inside you through memorization. The Psalmist David said, **"How can a young man keep his way pure? By living according to your word...Your word I have hid in my heart that I might not sin against you"** (Psalm 119:9,11). Hide the word of God in your heart and it will begin to change your habit of lying. The verses from the beginning of this chapter are a good place to start and will begin to change your tongue.

Give God time (Philippians 1:6)
Change takes time. Don't expect your speech to change completely overnight, although you can begin to change today. You have spent your whole life learning to lie well and you will need some time to change. **Philippians 1:6 says, "He who began a good work in you will carry it on to completion until the day of Christ Jesus."** Let Him begin that good work in you today.

ACTION ASSIGNMENT

1. Rate yourself in the following areas of truthfulness on a scale of 1-5 with 1 being "I don't struggle at all" to 5 being "a serious problem." Be as honest as possible!

	AREA	1	2	3	4	5
A	Direct lies (Openly saying things that you know to be false)	/				
B	Exaggeration ("Stretching" the truth to your advantage, adding to numbers or facts)		/			
C	"Children" lies (telling them untrue stories, calling them untrue names, threatening with untrue threats)	/				
D	False impressions (speaking things which allow others to believe something that isn't true.)			/		
E	Keeping Quiet (being quiet about something which leads people to the wrong conclusion)			/		
F	Lying to earn money (giving untrue reports about things to sell, lying to get a job)	/				

2. Reflecting on the above chart, which area is God speaking to you about? *feeling social pressure isn't a good excuse to lie* What steps do you need to take to change in this area? (You may review the steps to change at the end of the chapter.)

3. Reflect on the way your culture deals with truthfulness. In which areas does your culture tolerate lies? List at least three of them below. My culture encourages lies in the following areas:

    a. *weight*

    b. *age*

    c. *Social activism / involvement*

4. Now choose <u>one</u> of the areas you listed above. Which one did you choose? __*C*__ Give a concrete example of how this lie is expressed in the following areas:

    a. The political world

    making claims not backed by actions

    b. In families

    fighting or overhyping self involvemen

    c. In the church

    apathy or rage

    d. In the business world

    cancel culture

5. Think further about this area. What do you think is the root cause of this lie? In other words, what motivates people to do it? Try to dig below the surface cause.

    look good / appear "woke"

Chapter Seven

THE LEADER AND AUTHORITY

Jesse was a young man with zeal to serve the Lord. He felt called to preach and had visions of how God would use him to change the world with his messages. But his pastor didn't give him any opportunity to preach in the Sunday service and only allowed him to preach to the youth. Jesse felt slighted by his pastor and began accepting many invitations to preach in other places. God seemed to bless him and use his gifts primarily outside of his church.

After some time, he left the church and started his own ministry, taking several of the church members with him. Eventually he started his own church. For several years the new church flourished. The people recognized Jesse as a pastor and a man of God. But as time went on, some of the youth in the church did not respect his authority and began doing their own thing. He felt irritated and tried to encourage them to be committed to the church. The problem, however, continued to escalate and soon he realized that more than half of the youth had left the church.

What went wrong? Jesse was simply reaping what he had sown

in the realm of authority. Like many leaders, he did not have a good understanding of the spiritual issue of authority. Whether in the world of work or in the church we often view authority negatively. We want to be freed from its control. We like to be *in* authority but not *under* authority.

In this chapter I will look at the biblical view of authority and particularly at how it relates to leadership. I will focus on the teachings of the Apostle Paul, one of the greatest leaders in history.

Paul said in 1 Corinthians 11:1, "Follow my example, as I follow the example of Christ." In this short verse are packed powerful principles of Christian leadership and authority. This verse teaches that **leadership begins with following**. Paul says, "Follow me, as I follow." He could call others to follow him only because he was also following someone. It is ironic, but true, that *only those who follow are worthy to lead*. Ben Franklin said "He who cannot obey cannot command."[19] You cannot effectively be *in* authority if you are not *under* authority.

This is a strange concept. I thought I was a leader because I could make others follow me. But Paul was a leader because he was first of all a follower. He unashamedly told the Corinthians to follow him as he followed Christ. He could speak with authority because he was a man under authority. Paul recognized God's authority over him as well as the authority of the church. (See Acts 14:26-15:4 for two examples of Paul's submission to the churches in Antioch and Jerusalem.)

Too often we think negatively of persons in authority, as people who restrict us and tell us what to do. But as leaders, we must have a proper understanding of authority so that we can correctly use our positions of authority. Scripture provides four major principles of authority that every leader should understand.

Principle One: God Establishes Authority

We need to recognize the origin of authority. The Bible clearly teaches that God establishes all authority. God has not established

---

[19] Benjamin Franklin, *Poor Richard's Almanack, 1734.*

"some" authority, but "all" authority. Romans 13:1, says, "There is no authority except that which God has established." Authority is God's idea; it is His plan for each of us to be under authority. His universe is a place of order and there is always a chain of command that He established. If you want to experience peace in your life, you must first understand God's principles of authority and function properly within them. Paul continues by saying, "The authorities that exist have been established by God." What are these authorities? I believe that God has established four main areas of authority.

Home

In the home is the first and perhaps the most important area that God has established authority. Many family problems come from an improper view of authority. Scripture teaches that in the home, the man is the leader and that the wife is to submit to his authority. (It also teaches that the man is under the authority of Christ and should submit to Him. If men would submit to Christ, women would not have such a problem submitting to them.)

Parents hold authority over their children and God expects children to be obedient. Colossians 3:20 says, "Children obey your parents in everything, for this pleases the Lord." Whose responsibility is it to see that this verse is obeyed? I believe that it is the responsibility of the parents, not the child. One of the greatest things parents can do for their children is to teach them obedience and a proper attitude towards authority. When children fail to learn this lesson at home, they often cause problems in schools and in the work place. (For further study note the following scriptures: 1 Corinthians 11:3; Ephesians 5:21-33; Colossians 3:20, Ephesians 6:1-3, 1 Timothy 3:4, Proverbs 1:8; 3:1-2; 4:1-2; 6:20 23; 7:1-2; 13:1; 15:5; 23:22, Exodus 20:12.)

Church

God has also established church leaders to be in a position of authority. Hebrews 13:7 says,

> Obey your [church] leaders and submit to their authority. They keep watch over you as men who must give an account. Obey them so that their work will be a joy, not a burden, for that would be of no advantage to you.

Note the chain of authority in this verse: the people obey the leaders and the leaders are accountable to a higher authority. (See also 1 Thessalonians 5:12-13.)

In the church, God planned positions of authority such as pastors, elders, deacons, prayer leaders, small group leaders, youth leaders, etc. Every church of which I am aware has some hierarchy of authority. The titles may vary from church to church, but all have a chain of command.

> Many people don't want to join a church because they don't want to be under authority.

Many people do not want to join a church because they do not want to be under authority. They go to a church until they clash with the leaders; then they feel "called" to go to another church. Such "spiritual tourists" do not understand God's plan and will consistently miss the blessing that God had prepared for them.

If you are a church leader, recognize that God has both given you authority and placed you under authority. Notice that the verse in Hebrews says that leaders will also give an account. God's system always has an order and even the highest person in the denomination will still be held accountable for his leadership.

Government

Romans 13:1-7 clearly teaches that God has established your government and that He expects you to submit to it. This includes all elected and appointed officials. It includes the police officer and the tax collector.

Paul does not say that you should submit only when you agree with everything the government does, or if it has no corruption, but instead it simply says that you "must submit [yourself] to the governing authorities" (see also 1 Peter 2:13-14). This includes paying taxes, obeying the laws and respecting and submitting to those in authority.

This is a difficult teaching, especially for believers who live under a corrupt government system. It may help to remember that when Paul wrote these words he was in prison, detained by an unjust and corrupt government that killed many believers. Still, he expected submission to the government. Paul recognized that the government could keep him as a prisoner but he would still accomplish the purposes of God for his life. This does not mean that you must blindly agree with everything that happens in the government or keep quiet when you need to speak about injustices. It does mean that you should respect the authority of the people that God places in government positions.

Work/School

A final area that God has established authority is in the area of employment or education. Many of the principles given in Scripture for slave/master relationships apply to our places of employment or education. Principals, headmasters, teachers, bosses, CEO's, managing directors and supervisors are all in positions of authority.

God expects you to respect people in these positions, not based on the character of that person, but simply because he is in that position. 1 Peter 2:18 says, "submit...not only to those who are good and considerate, but also to those who are harsh." Paul gives special instructions to those working for Christian employers, "Those who have believing masters are not to show less respect for them because they are brothers. Instead, they are to serve them even better, because those who benefit from their service are believers, and dear to them. These are the things you are to teach and urge on them" (1 Timothy 6:2). For further study see: Ephesians 6:5 8; Colossians 3:22-25; and 1 Peter 2:18.

Principle Two: God Expects Submission To Authority

Because God has established authority, your response to it is crucial. You can respond to authority in your life in many different ways. You can **ignore it**. You can **rebel against it**. You can **run away from it** or you can **submit to it**. Which is the Christian way?

Many of the verses that I have already mentioned make it clear that *God expects you to submit* to authority. "Everyone must submit himself to the governing authorities, for there is no authority except that which God has established" (Romans 13:1-2).

What is submission? My definition of submission is: *to recognize and respect the authority of those over you and to willingly support their leadership.* Submission is not only an external compliance with the demands of authority, it is a heart attitude as well. Sometimes rebellion is done quietly, or even with the look of submission. It is possible to outwardly obey the *command* of the one in authority while inwardly refusing to recognize his right to give the order.

The story is told of a small child who had disobeyed his mother. As a punishment, she told him to sit on a stool for some time. Glaring at his mother, he grudgingly sat down and said, "I'm sitting down on the outside, but *inside* I'm still standing up!" External obedience does not equal submission.

Some believe that submission means *not disagreeing with an authority*. But I believe it is possible to respectfully disagree and to share my opinion in a proper way, while still recognizing the right of the person over me to make the final decision.

Many people feel submission is *a sign of inferiority or weaknesses*. This, however, is a distortion of true submission. Jesus, who voluntarily submitted Himself to the Father for the sake of accomplishing a divine plan, stands as the model for submission. As God, Jesus cannot be described as either inferior or weak, but He willfully submitted. David also modeled that a superior person sometimes must submit to an inferior person. He illustrated the importance of respecting authority (even unjust authority) when he submitted to King Saul, twice refusing to harm "the Lord's anointed" and waiting for God to remove Saul from power and give David the throne.

Submission is for your good

Because submission is commanded of God, it must also be good. Following are four of the benefits of submission, as outlined in scripture.

Submission places you under the protection of authority

When I submit to an authority, I come under the protection of that authority. Submission to authority is like an umbrella over my head that protects me from the rain and the hot sun. As long as I stay under it, I am safe.

According to biblical principles, people in positions of authority will be held accountable for those under them. Thus, you are protected when you are under authority. This protection may be legal, spiritual, physical or social protection.

One of the things that authority protects you from is **danger**. I have a son who is under my authority. I give him instructions and I expect him to obey me. Why do I do this? I do it because I want him to grow into a mature, responsible adult. I want him to learn some very important lessons in life. Sometimes I give him directions that are for his protection. I tell him "Don't play in the street." When he is older, I will tell him not to commit fornication. As long as he obeys me, he will be protected from danger. If he refuses to obey my authority, a car might hit him or he might get a sexually transmitted disease.

As long as he is under my authority, I am responsible for him and if he obeys, he will be protected. But if he rejects my authority then he will come under all sorts of temptations and circumstances that he is not able to overcome. He may feel that I am just trying to keep him from having fun. He may not understand what happens when a moving vehicle hits a child. If he rebels and disobeys, he will learn the hard way that rebellion is dangerous and leaves him unprotected.

A young boy in South America was playing under a large tree. His father, sitting nearby, called out to the son, "Come here my son." The son came immediately without questions. As soon as he came out from under the tree, a large python fell right on the spot where he had been playing. His prompt obedience saved his life.

When you submit to authority, you are also protected from **blame**. If the teacher tells you to clean the room and someone comes and questions, "Why are you doing that?" you can quickly tell them, "The teacher told me to do it." If your boss tells you to deliver a package, and while you are doing so a policeman questions what you are doing, you will simply say, "My boss told me to do this. Talk to him!"

God did not give authority to **dominate**, but to **protect**. In **Numbers 30:1-16** God gives instructions concerning those who make unwise decisions while under authority. If they are under authority, they are protected from the consequences of making mistakes, since those in authority over them are held responsible. Authority both directs and protects you. Learn to appreciate the benefit of authority.

This should not be mistakenly applied when you are asked to do something that is clearly wrong. Then you must obey "God rather than men" (Acts 5:29). But most of the time when you struggle with submission it is not an issue of God's command versus man's command. Usually, you just don't want to obey.

Submission provides freedom for God to shape your character

The second good thing that submission does for you is that it provides freedom for God to shape your character. God has many things that He wants to teach you, so that you will become more Christ-like. Often He chooses to use the authority over you to shape your character.

God may realize that you need more patience. He might use a parent or another authority figure to produce patience in you. When this authority says "no" to the thing that you want to do, God may be trying to produce patience in you. However, if you fail to see the potential for God's work in frustrating situations, you will be tempted to rebel against authority and miss the character building that God intended.

God may allow you to be under a difficult boss in order to develop perseverance in you. He may allow your parents to be tough with you so that you will learn to be submissive to the voice of the Holy Spirit. He can and will use any authority figure to develop your character. The writer of Hebrews states:

> Moreover, we have all had human fathers who disciplined us and we respected them for it. How much more should we submit to the Father of our spirits and live! Our fathers disciplined us for a little while as they thought best; but God disciplines us for our good, that we may share in his holiness (Hebrews 12:9-10).

Earlier, Hebrews 5:8 says of Jesus, "Although he was a son, he learned obedience from what he suffered." The writer goes on to say, "No discipline seems pleasant at the time but rather painful. Later on however, it produces a harvest of righteousness and peace to those who have been trained by it" (Hebrews 12:11).

Where does this discipline come from? It often comes from those in authority over you – the pastor, teacher, boss, or parent. When you submit to their authority, God will work through them to shape your character so that you better reflect Jesus.

Even when the authority is wrong, God can use them to shape you. When you are under a bad authority, such as an abusive husband or a corrupt official, God will even use their weaknesses to shape a godly character in you – if you yield to His plan. This is true whether the authority is a Christian or not.

this is dangerous :)

Many people miss this blessing because they refuse to submit to an authority. Maybe it is a mother or teacher, boss or a pastor. Have you decided that you know more than the authority? Have you chosen to go your own way? If you are in this position, you need to go to that person, ask them to forgive you and place yourself under their authority again.

Some time ago I received a letter from my niece, who is learning these lessons as a young woman. She was working as a volunteer in a Christian organization when she wrote these words:

> I've shared with some of you over the past months about some of the struggles in leadership here. A lot of it was my learning to walk humbly underneath leaders who weren't leading,…so that when I saw things that I believed God ached to do, and things that my heart yearned for, but things in which I had no power to do or act, I needed to wait. On God. To pray. To not speak. To pray. To pray.
>
> So I did. And six months of crying out to God for Him to change things…frustration, hurt, anger, etc… came to a head this summer…It was so hard to see clearly sometimes. Late into many a night, crying out on my bed for JESUS to move here,…and still He called me simply to worship, to praise and thank Him, and from that perspective receive His hope, perspective, and BELIEF for the situation.
>
> It's been by far my hardest struggle here, but one which has taught me more than I know. About God's anointed lines of authority, about submission, about trusting God… about waiting. I've learned in a deep way that "God's ordered ways are best." He puts His leaders in place and says to love and pray for them. Anything I do outside those safe lines of authority, He will not bless.

She continues the letter by writing about how God began to move and open doors for them in the ministry. Through this experience, she received God's training. Waiting for God to move in these times is hard and often very painful, but, "It produces a harvest of righteousness and peace for those who have been trained by it" (Hebrews 12:11).

Submission provides an opportunity for God to guide you
God often provides direction for your life through authority figures. You may easily miss the best path simply because you refuse to acknowledge authority and, therefore, miss their wisdom and insight. Instead, be reluctant to take action against the advice of those in authority over you.

Again and again the Scripture gives examples of authority figures giving advice or direction. Abraham helped Isaac find a wife in Genesis 24. Moses' father-in-law helped him with wise advice in Exodus 18:13- 24. Timothy received instruction in the ways of the Lord from his mother and grandmother (2 Timothy 1:5). Much of the teaching in the New Testament comes from Paul or another church leader giving instructions on how to live the Christian life. Listen to those over you.

After being a pastor for several years, I received an invitation to lead a new ministry, Centre for Christian Discipleship. After praying with my wife about it, we felt that it was the right direction for us to go. But I also went to several people that were in authority over me to seek their counsel. Each of them affirmed the step that we were ready to take. We sensed God's confirmation through their counsel and made the transition with great confidence that we were moving in the will of God.

Solomon understood this principle when he wrote, "The way of a fool seems right to him, but a wise man listens to advice. Listen to advice and accept instruction, and in the end you will be wise" (Proverbs 12:15 and 19:20).

Children, go to your parents for advice. Be ready to wait if they don't bless you in the step you want to take. Wait for their blessing before you get married or enroll in training. Wives, ask your husband, even if he is not a believer, for advice. God can guide you through his life. Men, find a wise person that you can go to for counsel. Seek advice before buying a property, starting a business or accepting a job offer. Many have learned the hard way that what seems good initially is not always wise. Young men, get counsel. Older men are not your enemies; they can give you guidance. Deliberately place yourself under authority.

Submission provides opportunity for God's anointing to flow through you

All sincere Christian leaders desire to be used by God. You want His anointing to flow through your life. But this will happen only when you recognize and submit to God's established chain of authority. God strongly emphasizes and honors authority.

The Old Testament illustrates that God's pattern of ministry is based on authority. Typically, God would use a prophet, seer or other authority figure to give a call to someone for ministry. Often he would be set apart for the divine calling through the application of oil. Only through the vehicle of human authority did the individual receive God's call and anointing for ministry. (See Exodus 28:41; 29:7; 1 Samuel 16:12; 1 Kings 1:34; 19:15; and 2 Kings 9:3-6 for a few examples.)

> Place yourself in a position of true submission in order to receive the anointing of God.

The connection between authority and the individual did not end when he received the anointing. Instead, God expected him to fulfill his call under the authority of the one who administered the call. And as long as he operated within his call and submitted to that authority, God prospered him.

In Israel, when a king stepped out of line, the person who had called him could come back and rebuke him. When Saul offered the sacrifice without Samuel, contrary to his orders, he paid dearly for his rebellion (1 Samuel 15:23-28).

The New Testament church continued a very similar pattern, often replacing the oil with the laying on of hands. Paul laid hands on Timothy and gave him the authority to go out and represent him to the churches (2 Timothy 1:6). Paul's blessing to Timothy released the gifts that God had placed in him. The Apostles in Jerusalem blessed and affirmed Peter's ministry to the Samaritans and Paul's ministry to the Gentiles. Paul felt accountable, not only to the Lord, but also to those that had sent him out. He reported back to the Apostles in Jerusalem and to the church in Antioch (Acts 11:18; 14:27; 15:4; 21:17-19).

God uses leaders who are properly submitted to authority. He cannot bless rebellion. Many business and church leaders are struggling in their work, trying desperately to do great things for God, but they have failed to recognize authority. Others are externally submitted to authority but inwardly they are just waiting for a good opportunity to leave. They struggle to obey the requirements of their leaders and don't fully support them financially or spiritually. In order for God's fullest blessing to flow, a leader must recognize and submit to God's appointed authority. **Place yourself in a position of true submission in order to receive the anointing of God.**

These are the positive things that happen to you when you obey God's command to submit. Let's also look briefly at what happens if you refuse to submit.

Lack of submission places you under the wrath of God

Rebellion against authority brings serious consequences. According to **Romans 13:1-2,** resisting the authorities is resisting something that God has established. It says those who rebel will "bring judgment upon themselves." 1 Samuel 15:23, "rebellion is like the sin of divination" (or witchcraft).

Why is rebellion so serious that it is compared to witchcraft? If you are involved in witchcraft, you expose yourself to direct attack from the enemy. You open the door and welcome his power and influence in your life. In the same way, if you rebel you remove yourself from God's ordained protection. You have come out from under the protection of the umbrella. Once you are not under God's protection, you are in the enemy's territory, where the enemy has permission and authority to attack you. That is why excommunication from the church is referred to as handing the person "over to Satan" (1 Corinthians 5:5).

Many believers think rebellion is a small issue that can easily be joked about. Comments like, "He can't tell me what to do!" or "I listen only to the Lord" may sound innocent, but they are deadly poison.

You may think that it does not hurt to speak evil about government leaders, your boss, your husband, your parents or the pastor. But God's word says that it a very serious sin. **Numbers 16** gives the account of the rebellion of Korah, when Korah and 250 men challenged the authority of Moses. Korah basically said to Moses, "You're not special. We can also do what you do." He did not recognize that Moses was God's appointed leader. The result? The death of more than 14,000 people. God does not appreciate disrespect toward His leaders!

Disrespect for parents is just as serious and is a violation of the fifth commandment (See Deuteronomy 5:16 and Ephesians 6:1-3). This commandment comes with a promise, "So that you may live long and it may go well with you in the land the LORD your God is giving you," and also an implied curse for disobedience. In **Deuteronomy 21:18-21** God commands the death penalty for a son who is rebellious against his father and mother.

This brings us to an extremely important principle in Scripture: **Your response to human authority is your response to God's authority.** Think about that very seriously. It is not possible to fully submit to God if you have not submitted to human authority. If you rebel against the policeman, you are rebelling against a God given authority. If you disobey your boss, you are disobeying God. If you refuse to obey the pastor, you are resisting God.

You may think, "I can't wait to get out from under authority." Or you may feel, "I can't wait to become a leader so I can give orders." Or, "I can't wait to become the CEO." I have news for you: **You will never**

be out from under authority – so get used to it. God will always bring another authority into your life to continue His work in you.

Lack of submission and obedience in your life will, therefore, bring serious problems. Rebellion will place you under the wrath of God and open the door to many problems in your life. Remember that the law of sowing and reaping teaches that a person will reap what he sows. If a person sows rebellion, he will also reap rebellion. Many people have refused to remain under authority and have started their own church or business. Later, they discover that those under them will not submit to their authority. They have only reaped what they sowed.

Listen to the wisdom of Solomon in Proverbs 5:11-14. "At the end of your life you will groan, when your flesh and body are spent. You will say, 'How I hated discipline! How my heart spurned correction. I would not obey my teachers or listen to my instructors.'" There are serious consequences for disobedience. The wrath of God will be upon those who resist authority.

Principle Three: God Enables You To Submit To Authority

It is often difficult to submit to authority, especially for young people. But God promises that He does not require more of you than you can do with His help. 1 Peter 5:5-6 exhorts, "Young men, in the same way be submissive to those who are older. All of you, clothe yourselves with humility toward one another, because, 'God opposes the proud but gives grace to the humble.'" God is able to give you the proper attitude toward the authority in your life. When you find yourself resisting authority, you need to remember that God will also oppose you in your rebellion, but that if you are humble, He will give you the grace that you need. Ask Him

> Only those who are under authority should be entrusted with authority.

for the grace to submit to the authority in your life. He will gladly provide it for you.

Why have I taken all this time talking about authority based on Paul's statement, "as I follow"? It is because, as a leader, you need to understand God's principles of authority so that you will have the right attitude toward those above you and those beneath you in terms of authority. **Only those who are under authority should be entrusted with authority.** The issue of authority is often very difficult to assess. How can you evaluate yourself and others in the area of submission?

Six tests of submission to authority

1. Submissive people receive correction

If you are a submissive follower, you will accept correction from an authority. You will operate out of a spirit of respect and humility. You can be told that you have made a mistake. Remember, as a leader, that you are also a follower. You are still learning and growing in Christ.

When someone comes to you and points out a mistake, how do you respond? Do you resist by defending yourself? Or do you submit and accept the correction? Your flesh can so easily rise up and say, "Who do you think you are to correct me? Do you think you're perfect? What gives you the right to point out my error?"

This does not mean that you have to be unquestioningly obedient. Sometimes your authority's correction will be wrong or misguided. But in every case your response should be one of humility and openness toward their correction.

Proverbs 15:31 says wisdom is a reward for those who listen to correction, "He who listens to a life giving rebuke will be at home among the wise." Do not foolishly dismiss the rebuke or council of others, especially of those who have more experience and greater authority.

2. Submissive people admit mistakes

If you are a follower, you will openly admit your mistakes. The world teaches that *leaders do not make mistakes, and if they do, they don't admit it*. But this attitude only breeds arrogant leaders who cannot submit to others. Such leaders believe they are accountable to no one. As a Christian leader, you should be able to say, "I am sorry, I was wrong."

3. Submissive people do not "lord it over" others (1 Peter 5:3)

We have already looked at Jesus' teaching on servanthood. A servant recognizes authority and is not, therefore, likely to abuse those under him. He will not demand or dictate. He will not use his position for personal gain. If you have the attitude of a follower, you will be less likely to abuse your authority in the lives of others. You will not try to dominate since you know that you are also a follower. Submission enables us to not "lord it over" others.

4. Submissive people make themselves accountable

Accountability is difficult for a leader unless he acknowledges that he is also a follower who is under another person's authority. A submissive person does not struggle to allow authority to hold him accountable. A worker who is submission will gladly provide an accurate report to the supervisor. A submissive wife does not have a problem sharing with her husband what she is doing or how she spent their money. A submissive youth leader does not wrestle with reporting his plans to the senior pastor. A submissive church member can easily approach the pastor to explain why she will not be at church on Sunday. A submissive pastor will not hesitate to give a report of his activities to his overseer or bishop. Every leader should be accountable to someone.

5. Submissive people are loyal

Those who submit to authority are loyal to that authority. Loyalty simply means that you are with your leaders, for better or for worse. It means that you will defend the reputation of your leaders and speak well of your organization.

Loyalty does not always mean agreement. Contrary to what the world models, you can disagree with someone who is over you and still be loyal. The world interprets any slight difference between the leader and the follower as betrayal and disloyalty. But no two individuals will always agree. As different people with different minds, we will see and understand things differently. Further, you should not even expect to agree with every decision made by your leaders.

> I can disagree with someone who is over me and still be loyal.

Loyalty means that when you disagree, you may respectfully share your view with the leader, but you must also be willing to obey if he does not change. I believe that openly and respectfully disagreeing with any authority shows more loyalty than secret disapproval. Some people will attend a meeting and keep quiet while decisions are made. Then afterwards they grumble and complain about the decisions. They will not be able to follow wholeheartedly. This is not only disloyalty but also rebellion. Either be loyal or leave the organization.

6. Submissive people show respect

The Bible says that you should "respect those who work hard among you, who are over you in the Lord" (1 Thessalonians 5:12). This verse talks especially about church leaders but applies to all in authority.

Leaders deserve respect. Leading is a difficult and demanding job. It calls for sacrificing of time and energy. Leaders have many meetings, people who need to be visited, and piles of other miscellaneous tasks. Leaders have to deal with all the needs the followers, which is often very tiring. You need to respect them by recognizing them for their hard work.

Not only do leaders deserve respect because of the difficulty of their task, but also because the Lord has given them a position of authority. That position does not mean that they are better or more educated than you. It simply means that you owe them respect because of the position they hold.

Without the respect of followers, effective leadership is nearly impossible. If you stop respecting your leaders you are plotting for their downfall. They need your respect. *Give it to them.* If you willingly choose to respect your leaders, they will be less likely to demand it from you.

1 Thessalonians 5:12 also says to hold your leaders in the highest regard in love. You are commanded to respect the position, regardless of the individual person who holds it. Again, this does not mean that you must agree with everything your leaders say. And you certainly should not overlook sin in their lives. But you must hold them in high regard. What does this mean and how can you do it?

a. Respect is shown by controlling your tongue

One of the best ways that you can respect authority is to **control your tongue**. Make a commitment that you will not speak evil of any of the leaders of your church, your home, your job and your country. You should be willing to make this commitment about anyone. Do not get together with others and compare leaders.

Do not talk negatively about the leaders of your church in front of your children. Some parents go home after church on Sunday and have "roasted Pastor" for lunch tearing down their pastor in front of their children. Those who speak evil about the leaders of a church do more damage than someone who might come with a bulldozer and tear down the walls. The same thing happens at many staff rooms or corporate water coolers.

b. Respect is shown by following willingly

You show respect for your leaders when you willingly follow their vision and direction. Do what is requested of you without resistance. If you oppose an idea, discuss it openly with your leader instead of pretending to agree and submit. It is very discouraging for a leader to work hard at a project with little or no support from his people.

Hebrews 13:17 says that you should obey your leaders so that their work will be "a joy, not a burden, for that would be of no advantage to them." Your leader will rejoice when you willingly follow and support him without grumbling, complaining or discouraging others.

Principle Four: God Exemplifies Submission To Authority

Not only does God establish authority, and expect and enable submission to authority, but He also gives us the fullest example of submission. He does this both through Christ and through Paul, who said, "Follow me as I follow Christ" (1 Corinthians 11:1).

Christ submitted to God

In all areas of your life Christ is the perfect model for you. Likewise, in this area of submission, you should imitate Christ. Paul made it clear that he followed Christ as the example for a life fully submitted to the Father. In Philippians 2:1-11, Paul paints a graphic picture of the details and results of Christ's submission.

Christ chose submission

Christ chose to submit. Paul states clearly that He did not consider equality with God something to be grasped. He could have demanded His rights, refusing to give up His position. But He chose to submit instead, voluntarily humbling Himself before the Father. Likewise, your submission is a choice. True submission is not forced upon you but is embraced willingly.

Christ submitted completely

When Christ chose to submit to the Father, He did not do so half-heartedly. He chose a submission that took Him all the way to the cross. But even before the cross, Christ's decision to submit to the Father's will was not easy. He first became a man, a humbling step that required Him to relinquish the power and privileges of His heavenly position. Not only did He become a man, but He also became a servant, the lowest position. Then He submitted to death, the most painful and humiliating death imaginable. In the garden, He won His final struggle with submission when He said, "Not My will but Yours be done" (Luke 22:42).

You must decide whether your submission will be complete or partial. You choose whether to follow with your whole heart or only with your lips. You decide whether you follow only when it is easy or whether you continue submitting when the demands become more difficult.

Christ's submission was rewarded

The beauty of Christ's submission is that He was richly rewarded for it. "Therefore God exalted Him to the highest place and gave Him the name that is above every name" (Philippians 2:9). Because He submitted and became a servant, God exalted Him. Jesus gave up His title but was later given the highest title. He abandoned His position only to receive the highest position. He bowed His knee in submission and one day every knee will bow before Him. He relinquished His authority and now we acknowledge His authority.

In your life as well, God will compensate you for genuine submission. As you truly submit, He will shape your character, test your heart, develop your calling and then use you in greater ways than you could have ever imagined.

When you struggle to submit, remember Christ. He did it and He lives as an example, guaranteeing that you can also submit. In all of life, and certainly in leadership, your goal should be to imitate Christ Jesus. You should want to become like Him in your thoughts, in your actions, in your words. He is your example of submission.

Paul submitted to Christ

Paul is another model of the beauty of submission. Paul says, "Follow my example as I follow the example of Christ" (1 Corinthians 11:1).

Paul does not say he followed Peter; he does not say he followed the example of James; he followed *Christ*. As a leader, you work under human authority and should be challenged by their lives, but your focus must be on Jesus Christ.

Remember, of course, that Paul clearly recognized both divine and human authority and he submitted himself to his earthly leaders. He reported regularly to his home church at Antioch and when a potentially divisive issue in the church arose, he submitted to the Council at Jerusalem (See Acts 15). Paul's life exhibits the same characteristics as Jesus' submission.

Paul chose submission

When Paul said, "I follow," he indicates a personal choice. Yes, Christ called him in a dramatic way, but Paul still had to choose to submit to that call. He chose to be "crucified with Christ" (Galatians 2:20).

Paul submitted completely

Paul completely committed himself to following the "example of Christ" (1 Corinthians 11:1). It became his life's passion to "know Christ and the fellowship of his sufferings" (Philippians 3:10). He was prepared to follow Christ to the point of death. In Acts 20:24, Paul said, "However, I consider my life worth nothing to me, if only I may finish the race and complete the task the Lord Jesus has given me – the task of testifying to the gospel of God's grace." That is total submission to the call of Christ.

Paul often referred to himself as a "servant of Jesus Christ." Paul defined himself as serving under the authority of Jesus. He could have boasted about his titles and positions, about the significant impact of his ministry, but choose instead to be the "least of the apostles" (1 Corinthians 15:9). This is complete submission.

Paul's submission was rewarded

Like Christ, Paul received a reward for his submission. This passage illustrates just two of the ways that Paul's submission received compensation.

1. Paul's life became a model

Because Paul served under authority, he could tell others to follow his example. Paul's life became a model for the early church and it still serves as a model for us today. He was not a leader who just told others what to do; he showed them with his life, which served as a powerful example because he became like Christ and submitted himself to Christ.

When you follow Christ, submitting to His authority and to human authorities, your life will become a model to others.

2. Paul's call became a method

Paul issued a call to the Corinthians to "follow me" (11:1). He challenged others to act, to move and to make progress. Leadership is the ability to influence others. You cannot call yourself a leader if you do not impact other people. In this passage, Paul the leader presents the call to those who follow him. In itself this is not significant; it is the context of his words that is significant. As Paul models in this passage, **the call to others must come *after* you provide an example from your own life and *after* you follow your own authorities.**

This is where many leaders make a mistake. They believe their position or title enables them to command others. They base their authority on position rather than on submission. But Paul's method teaches that *true authority comes only when we have learned the painful lessons of submission*. The leader's authority comes from a life that first focuses on God and submits to the authorities and second models a willingness to serve.

You will greatly influence the lives of others after you learn to follow authority and model a godly lifestyle. Only then can you expect others to follow you and call them to action. This then is the way to leadership: first submit yourself to God, then submit to those that He has placed in authority over you; live your life as a model to others and then call others to follow you.

Paul was rewarded for his submission. His submission gave him the power and authority to continue speaking to us today, many generations later. What is your response to authority? Are you submissive to those that are over you? Do you want to exercise authority without being under authority? Prayerfully review this chapter and allow God to deal with any rebellion in your heart. Go to those that you have rebelled against and ask their forgiveness. Completing the action assignment will help you continue to grow as a leader under authority.

ACTION ASSIGNMENT

1. List the people that are in authority over you in each of the following areas (put at least one person's name in each category):

Home	Church	Government	Work/School
Dylan	Ray	police	Dylan
	Josh	Bill Lee	Chris Moore
	Dean		
	Randy		
	Scott		

2. In which of these areas is it most difficult for you to submit?____
   ____Why?

   ~~home~~ & work — I don't often recognize a need for transparency

3. Review the teaching on the area that you chose in #2 above. Look up all of the Scripture references listed for that area and choose one of them to memorize. After you have memorized it, wait 24 hours and then say it to someone who can check it.

   Those who have believing masters should not be disrespectful to them because they are brothers, but should serve them better, since those who benefit from their service are believers & dearly loved.

4. Look at the six tests of submission to authority below and ~~rate~~ yourself by marking the appropriate box. Do you have no problem with this area? Do you sometimes have a problem? Or does this area need significant work?

Area of Submission	No Problem	Sometimes a problem	Much work needed
I am correctable		/	
I can admit mistakes			/
I do not "lord it over" those under me	/		
I am accountable to those over me	/		
I am loyal to those over me		/	
I am respectful to those over me	/		

5. In what way has God spoken to you about this area of authority?

I need more humility & admission of mistakes/wrong doing. I need openness to correction & to assume well of others

6. What practical steps can you take that will help you to improve in the area(s) in which you need improvement? (List the steps you may take. For example: talking to that leader over you and asking forgiveness, memorizing more Scripture on authority, changing the way you talk about people in authority, finding someone to be accountable to, etc. Don't say "I will pray about it" or "I will ask God to help me".)

Memorize scripture about correction

Put an "x" here after you have completed one of the steps you have written above. _____

Prov. 12:1 Whoever loves discipline loves knowledge, but he who hates reproof is stupid.

Chapter Eight

THE LEADER AND FORGIVENESS

Simon and Joshua were great friends. They spent as much time together as possible and enjoyed taking trips together. They challenged each other to keep growing in Christ and enjoyed several years of close friendship. Then Simon met a beautiful lady and soon they were engaged. Joshua felt jealous and refused to accept the new relationship. Soon he spread the word that Simon and his fiancée had slept together. When Simon heard what Joshua had done, he was furious and vowed to never forgive Joshua for his wrong. They parted ways and even after many years they have not forgiven one another.

Forgiveness. What a difficult word for Simon. For Simon and for every follower of Christ, the concept of forgiveness is easier to talk about than to practice. We love to be forgiven and rejoice that, in Christ, God has forgiven us of all of our sins. But how many of us can honestly say, "There is no one who has wronged me that I have not sincerely forgiven?" My goal in this chapter is to bring each of us to that point.

It would be wonderful if those who have been forgiven much would also forgive much. Sadly, this is not the case. Many, many believers, like Simon and Joshua, foster bitterness and unforgiveness throughout their lives. Lack of forgiveness is not only a sin, but also a crippling disease, especially for a leader.

Forgiveness is a word you may use a lot but whose meaning has often become unclear. What does it practically mean to forgive? The dictionary defines forgiveness: "To cease to feel resentment against an offender."[20]

Notice that this does not mean that what the person did to us was right. It only deals with your response to the offender. It is important to realize that forgiveness does not mean pretending that what the other person did is acceptable or that the person deserves forgiveness. Many people confuse these issues and refuse to forgive because it seems like the other person's wrong actions are being justified or excused when forgiveness is extended.

When you forgive, however, you transfer the responsibility for punishment to God. God will be responsible to deal with the other person; forgiveness is your responsibility. To forgive is a conscious decision that you can make. In my book *Free at Last* I give this operational definition of forgiveness:

> Forgiveness is a choice that we make; it is an act of our will; not our feelings. If you wait until you feel like forgiving you will never forgive. It is a choice that we choose to make on the basis of what God has done in forgiving us. It does not mean that we forget what has been done to us but that we set the other person free. They can no longer control us and bring confusion and pain to our lives.[21]

---

[20] In *Websters New Collegiate Dictionary*, 1977 ed., 451.

[21] Jon Byler, *Free at Last* (Nairobi Kenya: Centre for Christian Discipleship, 1997), 14.

Jesus teaches about forgiveness through the powerful story found in Matthew 18:21-35, the parable of the unmerciful servant. Take a moment and read it, since it is the biblical foundation for this chapter and a good illustration of what has happened to many Christians. Take a few minutes to reflect on the meaning of the story.

The story teaches that you have been forgiven of many sins. You are the servant in the story and God is the master. He has forgiven you for so many things that your debt has exceeded your ability to repay. But in his mercy, God has forgiven you.

How joyous the servant must have felt when he left the master's office debt-free. And how glad you were when you first realized that Christ forgave your sins. But if you fail to forgive another person, you become like the servant that choked the man who owed him money. And Christ will respond to you just as the master did in the story. He became very angry with the servant who refused to forgive his fellow man and had him tortured in jail.

With this story as a background, I will examine five Biblical principles of forgiveness.

The Requirement Of Forgiveness

Is forgiveness really a requirement for a Christian, or is it an option? Jesus' commands, his example and other scriptures make it clear that forgiveness is a requirement for all Christians.

The commands of Jesus

Jesus commanded you to forgive. I have already looked briefly at the parable of the unmerciful servant. Here I will note two of Jesus' additional teachings on this subject.

The first is found in the Lord's Prayer:

> Forgive us our debts, as we also have forgiven our debtors. And lead us not into temptation, but deliver us from the evil one. For if you forgive men when they sin against you, your heavenly Father will also forgive you. But if you do

not forgive men their sins, your Father will not forgive
your sins (Matthew 6:12–15).

This concept is so radical that people often try to find another
interpretation of the passage. Surely, Jesus did not mean it that way,
did He? But it is clear.

God will not forgive us if we do not forgive others

Tom Eliff says, "He who cannot forgive others breaks the bridge over
which he himself must pass if he would ever reach heaven; for every
one has need to be forgiven."[22]

A second place Jesus teaches clearly about the need for forgiveness
is in Matthew 5:23-24, "Therefore, if you are offering your gift at the
altar and there remember that your brother has something against you,
leave your gift there in front of the altar. First go and be reconciled
to your brother; then come and offer your gift."

This verse indicates that God is more concerned about your
relationships than your worship. He is not happy with lifted hands
and bitter hearts. He is not excited about tithes and offerings from
people who cannot love or even talk to each other. He desires a people
of forgiveness and reconciliation.

The example of Jesus

Not only did Jesus teach about forgiveness, He also demonstrated
forgiveness. The best example of this is His prayer from the cross,
"Father, forgive them, for they do not know what they are doing"
(Luke 23:34). It is not easy to forgive those who kill you. But Jesus
did and you are commanded to follow His example.

Other biblical commands

Other passages in Scripture also clearly command forgiveness. In
Romans 12:18 Paul writes, "If it is possible and as far as it depends on
you, live at peace with everybody." God does not hold you accountable

---

[22] Stan Toler, *Minute Motivators* (Tulsa, OK.: River Oak Publishing, 2002), 22.

for circumstances beyond your control but He holds you responsible to do your part to restore every relationship in your life. This involves either requesting or extending forgiveness.

Paul adds in Colossians 3:13, "Bear with each other and forgive whatever grievances you may have against one another. Forgive as the Lord forgave you." Again, Christ is your model of forgiveness and you are to do what He did. Similarly in Ephesians 4:32 Paul says, "Be kind and compassionate to one another, forgiving each other, just as in Christ God forgave you."

Clearly God requires you to forgive. It is not a suggestion or an item for prayer, but a command to be obeyed.

The Reason For Forgiveness

If the scriptural commands are not enough, the effects of unforgiveness provide some of the most compelling reasons to forgive. At least four areas of your life are affected when you fail to forgive.

Unforgiveness affects you spiritually

Your spiritual life is the first area affected by your refusal to forgive others. Forgiveness is primarily a spiritual act and it will, therefore, affect you spiritually. Unforgiveness affects your relationship both with God and with your enemy.

When you do not forgive others, God does not forgive you. This is a difficult truth, but it is clearly taught in Scripture. The servant in Matthew 18 lost the forgiveness of the master when he refused to forgive his fellow servant. Jesus said clearly in the Lord's Prayer, "If you forgive men when they sin against you, your heavenly Father will also forgive you. But if you do not forgive men their sins, your Father will not forgive your sins" (Matthew 6:14-15). That's a heavy price to pay.

Is it worth holding a grudge against someone else when it means that God will not forgive your sins? I don't know about you, but I want my sins to be forgiven!

Not only do you jeopardize God's forgiveness, through your unforgiveness, but you also give Satan an opening into your life. Any unconfessed sin gives Satan a legal foothold in your life. (See Ephesians 4:26-27 for an example of how it happens with anger.) 2 Corinthians 2:10-11 identifies unforgiveness as one of the schemes of the devil.

Paul says, "If you forgive anyone, I also forgive him. And what I have forgiven – if there was anything to forgive – I have forgiven in the sight of Christ for your sake, in order that Satan might not outwit us. For we are not unaware of his schemes."

What are the schemes of the devil? He desperately wants to keep you from forgiving others. When you allow unforgiveness in your heart, you give the devil a wide open door into your heart. After he is in, he begins to launch an arsenal of weapons against you that affect you in many other areas of your life. (See my book *Free at Last* for a more comprehensive explanation of this concept.)

Unforgiveness affects you physically

Unforgiveness also affects your physical body. The servant in Matthew 18 was physically thrown into prison to receive physical punishment. Unresolved anger towards another person is deadly poison to your body. S.I. McMillen and David Stern write, "Fits of anger can lead to gut-wrenching nausea, vomiting, cramping, constipation, and diarrhea…Long-term anger makes for a short-term life."[23] The human body simply is not designed to handle unforgiveness.

Unforgiveness affects you emotionally

Unforgiveness also affects your emotions. When you refuse to forgive, you enslave yourself to negative emotions like anger, jealousy and bitterness. The servant in Matthew 18 expressed these emotions by grabbing his fellow servant by the neck. He was angry and shouted threatening words to his debtor.

---

[23] S.I. McMillen, and David E. Stern, *None of These Diseases*, revised ed. (Grand Rapids, MI.: Fleming H. Revell, 2000), 206-207.

Hebrews 12:15 warns about bitterness, "See to it that no one misses the grace of God and that no bitter root grows up to cause trouble and defile many." A root of bitterness often springs from unforgiveness and if it is not removed it will "grow up" to produce more emotional problems.

Unforgiveness can sometimes lead to emotional depression. My wife and I knew a lady whose husband had travelled overseas and abandoned her and their children. Left alone to struggle for survival, she became very bitter toward her husband. She began to suffer from depression and the doctors put her on many different medications, some to make her sleep and others to help her while she was awake.

But after she gave her life to Christ, she realized that she needed to forgive her husband and she did. God immediately healed her of depression and freed her from the need for medication. Her friends were amazed at the transformation in her life. Her act of forgiveness had set her free and enabled her to be emotionally stable. (This does not imply that all depression comes from unforgiveness. Depression is a complex problem that can come from many emotional, spiritual and physical sources.)

Unforgiveness affects you socially

Unforgiveness also affects your relationships. Thousands of friendships around the world are broken today because someone failed to forgive.

Simon and Joshua are representatives of people found in churches and organizations all over the world, people whose friendships have been destroyed because of unforgiveness. Unforgiving relationships produce hypocrisy. Artificial greetings and plastic smiles replace genuine love. Hatred begins to solidify. You may not want to say that you hate someone, but if you are bitter towards him, then you do not love him.

You need to recognize that every healthy relationship will require a measure of forgiveness. No one is perfect and you will need to extend forgiveness to everyone with whom you desire to remain in fellowship.

All these results of unforgiveness may be what Jesus referred to when He said that the person who failed to forgive would be handed over to the "tormentors" or "to be tortured" (Matthew 18:34, KJV and NIV). Bitterness will torture you. Many people live in incredible amounts of bondage because they refuse to forgive.

Lack of forgiveness cripples a Christian spiritually, physically, emotionally and relationally. When you refuse to forgive it is as though you carry the offense around on your back. You hold an ever expanding sack full of grievances that weigh you down, keep you awake at night and burden you during the day.

When your brother offends you, you throw him in the sack. When your neighbor annoys you, he goes in the bag. When your parents mistreat you, you add them to your collection. The bag becomes heavier and heavier. It troubles you in your sleep. While walking, it brings you low and slows you down because you keep remembering what all those people did to you. It is an unnecessary burden and Christ wants to set you free. To help remove the burden, let's examine the rules of forgiveness.

The Rules Of Forgiveness

By this point, I believe you have seen the need for forgiveness. In this section I will examine the people to forgive, the things to forgive, the time to forgive and the frequency to forgive.

The people to forgive

Who do you forgive? It is easy to say "everyone" – which is the correct answer— but it will be more helpful to look at several specific people or groups of people that you need to forgive.

1. Yourself

You can easily overlook the first, and often the hardest, person that you need to forgive – yourself. Your past may be littered with major mistakes you have made, choices you regret, or evil that you have done to yourself and to others. When you dwell on all these sins, you blame yourself and give the devil an opportunity to make you carry a burden that is no longer yours.

Realize you are now a new creation and the Bible says that there is no condemnation to those who are in Christ Jesus (Romans 8:1). Do not carry guilt from the past. Refuse to look at any events from your past apart from the blood of Christ. Reflect on the following verses and then forgive yourself:

> Romans 8:1, "Therefore, there is now no condemnation for those who are in Christ Jesus."

> 1 John 1:9, "If we confess our sins, He is faithful and just and will forgive us our sins and purify us from all unrighteousness."

> Psalm 103:12, "As far as the east is from the west, so far has he removed our transgressions from us."

2. Your family

Your family members are also high on the list of people who need your forgiveness. Living closely with imperfect people will provide many opportunities for forgiveness. An East African proverb says, "When two axe heads are in the basket, they are bound to knock each other."

Forgive your **parents** for wrongs that they did to you when you were growing up. Maybe they disciplined you harshly or embarrassed you in front of your friends. Perhaps they called you unkind and untrue names. Maybe they didn't pay school fees for you or favored another sibling over you. Forgive them.

Forgive your **in-laws**. Perhaps they talk negatively about you or make your life difficult. Get them off your shoulders. Forgive them.

You need to forgive your **spouse**. This is a tough one. Daily your spouse can do things that offend you or irritate you. But you need to forgive him or her.

Once, while serving as a pastor, my wife and I went to counsel a couple having marriage problems. When we were ready to discuss the issue I asked the wife to begin. She started, "It was in 1988, June 14th, when my husband did this…in 1990 on October 30th, he made another mistake…on April 10th the following year he did…." She literally recited to us a long list of grievances. It was obvious that the first thing their marriage needed was forgiveness.

Parents also need to forgive **children**. When they do something wrong, discipline them appropriately and then forgive them. Sometimes while disciplining, a parent brings up an old list of the child's wrong doings together with the current failure. This shows that they were never truly forgiven. You need to remember that when you discipline your children they are not your enemies but your own flesh and blood.

Your children may believe that you hate them if you have not expressed forgiveness. The story is told of a child who was spanked and then asked to eat in the corner by himself. As the family said their prayers for the food, they heard a small voice from the corner also praying, "Lord, I thank you that you prepare a table for me in the presence of my enemies." It is good, after disciplining your children, to remind them verbally, "I forgive you."

You may also need to ask for forgiveness *from* **your children** when you wrong them. That's difficult for any parent but all parents make mistakes. Your children recognize your errors and wonder whether you will be strong enough to admit that you were wrong and ask for forgiveness. How powerful it is for a father to say, "I'm sorry, son, that I was angry at you, will you forgive me?" Try it! It is a beautiful thing to have a home where children have learned from a young age to extend, as well as receive, forgiveness.

3. Your friends

Certainly you have friends who have offended you at some point during your relationship. No matter who they are, sooner or later something will happen to strain the relationship. Maybe you told your friend something very personal and he told someone else. Now when you see each other you give a plastic smile and a limp handshake, but on the inside you carry a grudge. The relationship is dead, and you do not even want to restore it. Let go, forgive and let God restore your relationship.

4. People from past relationships

You may have received wounds from people in the past. Friends, relatives, boyfriends or girlfriends, classmates, teachers, or neighbors all may have hurt you. You no longer see them, but you still carry them on your back.

Before our marriage, my wife Loice prayed for a husband and specifically for a pastor. She became excited when a young man from Bible school showed interest in her and over time they

> As painful as it is forgiveness will set you free from the past.

developed a friendship. Letters passed back and forth and several visits took place. Then, with no explanation, the letters stopped. She never heard another word from him. Months passed and she became bitter. Any time she would drive past his area, her stomach would tighten. When she heard his name, her emotions were stirred.

Many years later, after she was happily married, she woke up in the middle of the night and realized that she still carried this man on her back. God spoke to her and asked lovingly, "Do you want that man from the past or the husband who is sleeping beside you?" "This one," she replied. "Then let that man go." She forgave the man, released another burden from her past and was instantly free. Through intriguing circumstances later, God brought her face to face with this man and she was able to talk to him with no malice. Years later, our son, not knowing what happened in the past, became friends with this man's son and brought him to our home for a weekend! Thankfully the past had been healed.

Some past memories are very painful. Perhaps you loved someone and had a child out of wedlock. Every time you look at the child it reminds you of the pain of that past relationship. Let God change that today so that the next time you look at that child you will see God's love and His grace, which delivered you from your old lifestyle and freed you from your guilt.

Some have experienced traumatic physical or sexual abuse and carry a deep scar. These wounds remain raw and extremely painful, even after many years. Often the victim cannot even talk about what happened. But Christ offers hope for these situations too. As painful as it is, forgiveness will set you free from the past. If needed, don't hesitate to seek professional counselling to find complete freedom from these memories.

5. Other Christians

Yes, other Christians need your forgiveness. We wrong each other in the things we do or say and we need to forgive each other. You may have been hurt by a Christian leader and are still carrying the wound from that experience. Or perhaps it was a fellow choir member, or a member of a small group who offended you. Colossians 3:13 instructs us, "Bear with each other and forgive whatever grievances you may have against one another. Forgive as the Lord forgave you." Do it now!

6. Non-Christians

Think about your relationships with non-Christians. They also may offend you, sometimes specifically because of your faith. What happens to your testimony when you refuse to forgive? On the other hand, when you say to a non-Christian, "I have forgiven you," you powerfully testify about the love and grace of God.

Romans 12:18 says, "If it is possible, as far as it depends on you, live at peace with everyone." How will your non-Christian friends and neighbors come to know Christ if you do not live out Christ's love and forgiveness before them and to them? Their eternal salvation is much more significant than your personal offense.

7. Those under your leadership

As a leader, you will have many opportunities to forgive. Many people will wrong you. Some will disappoint you. Some will gossip about you and spread false reports. Others will misunderstand your motives. Some will rebel against your leadership. As a leader, you cannot afford to carry the emotional baggage of unforgiveness. It will kill your ministry. You cannot effectively lead people that you have not forgiven.

As a leader you also need to help others learn to forgive. But you must first model it in your own life. Only when you live a life of forgiveness will you be able to help people obey Jesus' instructions:

> "Therefore, if you are offering your gift at the altar and there remember that your brother has something against you, leave your gift there in front of the altar. First go and be reconciled to your brother; then come and offer your gift" (Matthew 5:23-24).

Eugene Habecker states, "A leader who has not learned to be a good forgiver will not be as effective a leader as one who has. Leadership affords too many uncomfortable incidents, too many inaccurate accusations, and too little time to keep track of everyone who has 'wronged' you."[24]

What people in your life do you need to forgive? Reflect on the list of people in this section. If you are like most people, you will find that you have some people on your back who need to be forgiven.

---

[24] Eugene B. Habecker, *Rediscovering the Soul of Leadership* (Colorado Springs, CO.: Victor Books, 1996), 138.

The things to forgive

What do you forgive? Are some items outside the scope of your ability to forgive? Paul answers these questions in Colossians 3:13 where he says, "Bear with each other and forgive whatever grievances you may have against one another. Forgive as the Lord forgave you." The command clearly says you are to forgive "*whatever* grievances you may have". That is pretty comprehensive. In other words, it does not matter what someone has done; it can be forgiven.

Corrie Ten Boom suffered much under the Nazi regime. Her father and sister both died in concentration camps and she suffered great physical and emotional pain at the hands of the guards. After her release, she spoke about her experiences around the world and encouraged others to forgive. After one such meeting, she was greeting people and saw a man coming towards her in the line. In a flash she recognized him as one of the guards responsible for her suffering. He extended his hand and asked for her forgiveness. Her inward struggle lasted for seconds as she stood face to face with her painful past. But she realized that Christ's command applies to every situation, so she extended her hand to that man and together they experienced the grace of God.

Never allow yourself to say, "What he/she did to me is too much to forgive." God will never expect from you more than you are able to do with His grace.

The time to forgive

"When is the right time to forgive?" Do you forgive before or after the person has come to ask for your forgiveness? Should you allow the other person to suffer for a little while before you forgive?

When did Jesus, your example, forgive you? He died for your sins *before* you knew Him, *before* you realized what sin is or even how to repent. He was ready and waiting for you to come to Him and He had already forgiven you. Since you should be like Christ, you should forgive *before* the other person asks for your forgiveness. In many cases, they will never ask but you can still extend it to them without their permission.

One day my wife and another lady had a disagreement. In the process, my wife said some wrong things to this lady and later she felt convicted of her sin. She called the lady and asked for forgiveness. She was shocked at the reply, "I already forgave you." My wife learned a lesson that day that she has never forgotten. Whether or not someone comes to ask for your forgiveness, you should have a forgiving heart. Every time is the time for forgiveness.

The frequency to forgive

How many times do you forgive? What happens if someone repeatedly offends you? Is there a limit?

Peter asked Jesus a similar question in Matthew 18:21-22.

> "Then Peter came to Jesus and asked, "Lord, how many times shall I forgive my brother when he sins against me? Up to seven times?" Jesus answered," "I tell you, not seven times, but seventy-seven (seventy times seven, KJV) times."

Peter thought he was being generous by offering forgiveness up to seven times. He was probably shocked at Jesus' response, which indicated that he should forgive up to 490 times. But Jesus' point was not that you should be keeping a notebook with 490 marks as a record. The idea of keeping track that long is ridiculous. Instead, Jesus was saying, "Don't keep records!"

Paul said that love "keeps no record of wrongs" (1 Corinthians 13:5). What a powerful statement. Throw away the record book. Keep forgiving. When you find yourself thinking, "I forgave him a week ago and he doesn't deserve it again," remember how many times the Lord has forgiven you. So, what are the rules for forgiveness? **Forgive *everyone*, for *everything*, *now* and as *often* as the offense is repeated!**

The Results Of Forgiveness

What happens when you practice forgiveness? At least five positive things happen when you forgive.

Reconciliation with God

The first and most important result of forgiveness is that your relationship with God is restored. Your sins against God will be forgiven as you forgive others. I have already highlighted the Lord's Prayer, which says clearly:

> Forgive us our debts as we also have forgiven our debtors. And lead us not into temptation but deliver us from the evil one. For if you forgive men when they sin against you, your Heavenly Father will also forgive you but if you do not forgive men their sins, your Father will not forgive your sins (Matthew 6:12-14).

When you release forgiveness to others, God releases forgiveness to you. What a joy it is to have your sins forgiven and your record clean before God.

Reconciliation with others

Forgiveness also brings reconciliation with others. God can bring incredible healing to relationships when you practice forgiveness. It may not always be possible for the relationship to be healed, since the other person also has a choice, but when you take the initiative to forgive, you open the door for reconciliation. Too often one person waits for the other person to do something, and as long as both parties are waiting, nothing happens. Thousands of relationships have been restored because one person took the initiative to forgive. The courage to bring the issue into the open and to allow Christ's forgiveness to flow provides powerful medicine for broken relationships.

Christian growth

Forgiveness will also produce Christian growth in your life and character. When you forgive, you are being obedient to God's word and becoming more like your Heavenly Father. Paul says in Ephesians 4:32, "Be kind and compassionate to one another, forgiving each other, just as in Christ God forgave you."

If you carry people on your back because of unforgiveness, you will not be growing as a Christian. The weight of unforgiveness will hold you down and not allow you to progress in your spiritual life.

Hebrews 12:1 says, "Therefore, since we are surrounded by such a great cloud of witnesses, let us throw off everything that hinders and the sin that so easily entangles, and let us run with perseverance the race marked out for us." Unforgiveness is one of the sins that a believer must throw off to be successful in running the race.

In this same passage, the writer of Hebrews continues to say, "Make every effort to live in peace with all men and to be holy; without holiness no one will see the Lord. See to it that no one misses the grace of God and that no bitter root grows up to cause trouble and defile many" (Hebrews 12:14-15).

Until you can forgive those who have wronged you, you will not be able to love others as Christ loves you. Forgiveness is, therefore, an important step in Christian growth and one that every believer should take often.

Strengthened prayer life

Forgiveness also yields a stronger prayer life. Often, when you have unforgiveness in your heart, thoughts of the person of people you are bitter toward intrude on your prayer times. Although you may try to forget about the incident, the person keeps showing up. Just as a police roadblock on the road prevents vehicles from passing, bitterness hinders your communication with God.

Mark makes this connection when he gives us Jesus' words, "And when you stand praying, if you hold anything against anyone, forgive him, so that your Father in heaven may forgive you your sins"

(11:25). If you hold bitterness against someone, your prayers will not be effective. But when you forgive that person, the roadblock is removed and you again have free access to God in prayer.

Think about your prayer life. Have you allowed anyone to block your connection to God? Forgive that person and you will experience a new freedom in prayer.

Freedom from negative emotions

Finally, forgiveness will set you free from negative emotions. As noted earlier, unforgiveness takes a heavy toll emotionally, producing anger, resentment and bitterness. When you forgive this burden is rolled off of your shoulders, releasing the tension felt in your body. Many people cry during the process of forgiveness, as the pain and struggle are released.

Forgiveness is a powerful medicine for the body, soul and spirit, yielding wonderful results. You would think, then, that the church would be a place where people are eager to forgive. Instead, bitterness and broken relationships are some of the greatest problems facing the church. In the next section we will look at why it is so difficult to forgive.

The Resistance To Forgiveness

Forgiveness is difficult because it resists the natural inclinations of your flesh and culture.

Your flesh resists forgiveness

Your flesh hates to forgive others. By flesh I mean your natural, sinful self that is in rebellion against God. Your **pride** stands in the way of forgiveness. When I sin my pride does not want me to confess my sin and ask for forgiveness. When someone sins against me, my pride demands that the offending party pay dearly for his mistake.

Self-justification also hinders forgiveness. I can easily justify my own actions, believing I have very good reasons to refuse to forgive.

"Well, he shouldn't have said that!" or "I didn't start the argument, he did!" "He should come to me if he wants forgiveness." These are all examples of self-justification.

It is very easy to see another person's sin and very difficult to see your own. Jesus knew this when He said:

> Why do you look at the speck of sawdust in your brother's eye and pay no attention to the plank in your own eye? How can you say to your brother, 'Let me take the speck out of your eye,' when all the time there is a plank in your own eye? You hypocrite, first take the plank out of your own eye, and then you will see clearly to remove the speck from your brother's eye (Matthew 7:3-5).

How easily my sin looks like a speck, while others' looks like a beam. Because I can see my own motivations, from my perspective my actions seem right. If I have broken the law, at least I have a good reason for it. Certainly I deserve an exception because of my circumstances. But when I see another person do the exact same thing, I demand justice!

Likewise your flesh also very quickly and skilfully uses **blame.** Unfortunately, blame comes naturally, originating in the Garden of Eden. When God confronted Adam and Eve about their sin, Adam blamed Eve and Eve blamed the snake. You have inherited the tendency to blame from them and you probably do it very easily.

Usually my natural tendency is to believe that the other person is 90 percent wrong and that I am only 10 percent or less to blame. Since the other has committed the greater wrong, I justify refusing to deal with my 10 percent and blame the other person. Marriage helped me learn this lesson. Many times, when I had a conflict or disagreement with my wife, I would justify myself and blame her. "I said that because of the way she replied to my question. She shouldn't have looked at me that way."

I had to learn that even if I am only 10 percent wrong on an issue, I should still take responsibility for my part and deal with it properly.

By the way, there were very few times that I was only 10 percent wrong, usually my part was a lot bigger than that!

Your culture resists forgiveness

Forgiveness is also difficult because your culture resists it, reinforcing your inherited tendency toward sin. All cultures express the sin of unforgiveness, sometimes in very different ways. Which of the following statements or expectations are found in your culture?

"Men should never say, 'Sorry.'"

"Leaders should be powerful and never ask for forgiveness."

"People will not respect you if you ask forgiveness."

"People will see your weaknesses if you request forgiveness."

"Don't admit mistakes unless you are found out."

"Forgiveness is for cowards."

While some or all of these statements may seem normal to you, God wants something better. He wants you to forgive as He does because you have become a member of a new culture.

The Bibles says that the church is "A chosen people, a royal priesthood, a holy nation [this is culture], a people belonging to God" (1 Peter 2:9). Forgiveness is an integral part of the new culture that you joined when you gave your life to Jesus Christ.

Who are you carrying on your back? It is time to release them through the power of forgiveness. Spend some time alone in prayer, completing the action assignment, which provides practical steps that you can take in order to practice Christ's command to forgive. Do not move on to the next chapter before completing the questions. Before I wrote these words, I paused to pray for you. I asked God to set you free from all unforgiveness as you read these words, believing that you will start a new chapter of growth and freedom in your life. God bless you!

ACTION ASSIGNMENT

1. Take 10 minutes in prayer to examine your life. (Do this in a quiet place without any distractions.) Review the section: "The Rules of Forgiveness." Read the list of different categories of people that you need to forgive. Ask the Holy Spirit to reveal to you any people that you have not forgiven. Write their names here: *FBC leaders*

Zach V. & whoever was behind him
Hunter's ill assumptions
Rebecca Spoon's attitude // H.S. kids leaving me out
— Chelsea)
Lana's not sleeping
— FGC
Maria not responding/caring
— Magnon, Mallory, girl scouts

2. Forgive each one individually. Do this one by one in <u>audible</u> prayer. Tell God, "I forgive _____ (name of person) for _____ (what they have done against you.)." Note: This may bring out a lot of pain if the memories are deep but this is a part of the healing process.

   Put an "x" here when you have done this. _____X_____

   How do you feel now?

   "lighter" in some ways but now my neck hurts from the stress of thinking on those things

3. If you have offended them or if they are aware of the broken relationship, go to them personally and ask for their forgiveness. Start with the one that is most difficult.

   Put an "x" here when you have done this. _____

   What were their responses?

4. What beliefs or fears have kept you from forgiving others or asking for forgiveness in the past?

   believing I deserve to hear them ask for forgiveness/repent

5. What is God teaching you about forgiveness through this lesson and through the actions that you have taken?

   I have had much more bitterness and/or unforgiveness in my heart than I thought I did

Common questions about forgiveness

Forgiveness is difficult and sometimes we are willing to do so, but struggle with the practical steps to take. Because forgiveness deals with relationships with others it requires wisdom to know what God is asking you to do. Below are some common questions about forgiveness and suggested answers.

1. How do I know if I need to talk to another person? If the other person is aware of how they have hurt you or how you have hurt them, it is advisable to talk to them in person or in writing. Since God has spoken to you about this issue, it is your responsibility to take the initiative. Pray and ask God for direction and the right timing. If the other person is not aware of your hurt, it is possible that your confession would generate more problems than necessary in the relationship. If you feel that you have wronged the other person, even if your part is very small, it may be appropriate to ask forgiveness for that part without mentioning what they have done that hurt you. In this case, be very sensitive to what God will guide you to do and where helpful ask a trusted spiritual advisor for counsel without going into all the details.

2. What do I do if the person does not accept my forgiveness? Recognize that God only asks you to take care of your part in extending forgiveness or asking forgiveness from another person. Their response is not your responsibility. Of course, you want them to respond in a good manner, but that is outside of your control. Paul says, "If it is possible, as far as it depends on you, live at peace with everyone." (Romans 12:18) You do what you can do and leave the rest to God.

3. What if I am unable to contact the person I need to forgive or ask forgiveness? If you no longer know where the other person is it may not be possible to speak with them or write to them. However, do your part to forgive them and ask God to bring you back into contact with that person if He wants you to speak to them. You might be amazed at what happens! If the person is no longer living, it is more difficult since there is no hope of ever speaking to them. A couple of options may be helpful. You may be able to speak or write to someone who was close to that person and express your request for forgiveness to them. Or it may be helpful to either write a letter to that person or go to their grave side and speak your forgiveness. A trusted counselor may also help you to express your feelings and find relief from the pain in this situation.

Chapter Nine

THE LEADER AND FAMILY

David was voted "most likely to succed" when he graduated from business college with honors. He was passionate about serving God with his life and felt a clear call to the world of business. Soon after graduation he married a long-time friend Rose and soon launched his first business. He poured his life into building his business and worked long hours to make it succesful. Three children were born during those early years and with each one David felt more keenly his responsibility to provide for them. Every Sunday they went to church together as a family.

His hard work began to pay off as the business grew and David was grateful that God enabled him to provide for his family. But the success required even more time and frequent road trips away from home. He seldom arrived at home before the children were in bed and missed most of the their events at school.

When Rose suggested that they share more time together he reminded her that God called him to be the provider for the family and that he was working hard to meet their needs. He also reminded her that the growth of his business means that they have been able to generously support their local church as well as a missionary family. Further, his role as an elder enables him to bless the church with his leadership abilities.

Rose tries her best to understand and to be supportive but she finds herself slowly losing interest in the things of God. She feels like her life is drifting along without focus. She longs for the intimate relationship that she dreamed of having with her husband but she feels guilty for pulling him away from his work.

David's family is typical of many Christian leaders who feel torn between their call to be leaders and their responsibility to their family. Those involved in church leadership face the added challenge of balancing their God-given *call*, the daily demands of their ministry, and the expectations of their members with the needs of their family. Further, they can mistakenly interpret Jesus' command to "seek first the kingdom of God" (Matthew 6:33) as a call to give church work priority over family.

But God has a solution to this leadership dilemma. A key verse for understanding God's plan for the leader and his family is found in Paul's instruction to Timothy concerning the qualifications for church leaders. Paul says, "He must manage his own family well and see that his children obey him with proper respect. (If anyone does not know how to manage his own family, how can he take care of God's church?)" (1 Timothy 3:4-5). From this passage I have drawn 3 crucial principles for Christian leaders.

Principle One: Family Leadership Is A Prerequisite For Christian Leadership

Paul says that *before* a person is qualified to be a Christian leader, he "must" manage his own family well. Good leadership at home is a requirement for a Christian leader. (I do not believe this disqualifies a single person from being in leadership, but it is assumed that most leaders will be married.) On the other hand, a home that is out of control disqualifies one from leadership in the church.

This means that no matter how gifted an individual might be, if his family life is not in order, then he is not qualified to be in a position of leadership. Before a church chooses a leader, they should scrutinize his family life, evaluating whether his relationship with his wife is strong and growing and whether his children are under control.

Principle Two: Family Leadership Is Preparation For Christian Leadership

Paul says that the leader must manage his own family well before he can be ready to manage God's people. In other words, *before* a man can be a good leader in church or in other areas of his life, he must be a good leader at home. In fact, learning to lead his wife and children is preparation for other leadership roles. In many respects, the way that a man leads his family will be the way that he leads others whether in church or in his work. If he is harsh and abusive with his children, he will treat his followers the same way. If he belittles his wife with his tongue, he will likely do the same to those under his leadership. If his family finances are not controlled, he will be unlikely to properly handle the money of the church or business.

Principle Three: Family Leadership Precedes Christian Leadership

These first two principles lead to a third. Leadership in the home comes *before* leadership in other realms including the church. This is an issue of priorities. **God's call to work never comes before God's call to family**. God placed us first in families and then in work.

Pastors often misunderstand Matthew 10:37 where Jesus said, "Anyone who loves his father or mother more than me is not worthy of me; anyone who loves his son or daughter more than me is not worthy of me." Here Jesus says that family relationships should not come before your relationship with *Him*. This verse has nothing to do with the relationship between work/ministry and family. Combining these two teachings from Jesus and Paul, provides a framework for establishing the following priorities for a Christian leader:

- First, the leaders' relationship with God
- Second, the leaders' relationship with family
- Third, the leaders' relationship with work/ministry

I cannot overemphasize the importance of setting and observing these priorities in the life of a Christian leader. Clearly, nothing should come before a leader's relationship with God. Most leaders recognize that this comes first, but they often confuse the next two. Family, not work, should be the second most important priority for the leader even if the work is church work.

This has enormous practical implications for the everyday life of a Christian leader. It means that your family is more important than your followers. You must first ensure that the needs of your family are met before attending to the needs of those with whom you work.

> If your work is keeping you away from home every evening of the week, then something is wrong!

If your work is keeping you away from home every evening of the week, then something is wrong. You may need to resign from a committee delegate something or reduce your hours. Regardless of what you change, you must change something because you are cheating your family. That is a strong statement but I believe it with all my heart.

You are modeling God to your children through the way that you parent them. Make sure you are modeling for them the kind of God who takes time to be with them, play with them and learn with them, not one who is always leaving.

How does this apply to an unmarried leader? Although your commitments are not the same as a married leader's, family relationships are still an important part of your life. Consider how your lifestyle affects your family, how it represents God to them. What do you say about God's character if you are so busy for Him that you never have time to visit your family?

God has placed you in a family for a purpose. What a beautiful thing it would be for you to go to your mother one day and offer to help her work in the kitchen as a way of expressing the love of Christ to her. Instead of just praying for your family, perhaps God wants you to simply be with them sometimes. God desires to use you as an incredible witness and blessing to your family, as a representative of His love. They are your first calling.

In addition to the teaching of Paul I believe your family should be your priority for several other reasons. First, **God established the family from the beginning of human history to be the foundation of all of society.** In the home children first learn about God and learn the foundational elements of Christian lifestyle: respect for authority, obedience, service, good manners, courtesy, how to work, how to manage money, how to relate to society, how to respond to temptations, etc. These things are of great value to God and He has established the family for these and other purposes.

When something goes wrong in the family, things will go wrong in the society and in the church. Disobedient youth, teenage pregnancies and rioting college students are products of unhealthy families. Christian leaders should be a part of the solution to these problems by establishing strong Godly families.

Families should also be a priority because **a strong family enables the leader to minister effectively**. The strong support of a spouse and children makes work a joy whether the leader is called to church work or another vocation. With my families' support I can stand confidently before a congregation because I know that my wife will speak the first, "Amen" to my message. On the other hand, if my family life is not strong, I have no power or ability to counsel a struggling couple or a family.

It is incredibly difficult to leave home after an unresolved argument and to preach with anointing and authority in the church. I know; I've tried it! I soon learned, however, that it is worth all the time and effort needed to settle things at home before I try to minister to others. When I have the blessing of my wife to go and minister to others, I can walk with my head held high. But if I know that I have missed supper and time with the family, and that they are not happy about it, I will not even enjoy going home. My family's support makes all the difference in my ministry.

I have heard of many preachers who faithfully served the Lord but who neglected their families. Many of them, later in life, said with tears in their eyes, "I wish I had spent more time with my children." Likewise many business men and professional leaders lament the cost of focusing on vocational success at the expense of their family.

If you are so involved in your work that your children suffer for it, then you need to reevaluate what you are doing. Children quickly begin to resent the fact that Dad always has time for someone else but never time to play with them. This resentment turns to bitterness toward the God you are serving, since He seems to be monopolizing your time and affection.

The story of Eli in 1 Samuel 2-4 shows how easily a man who is serving the Lord can loose his family through neglecting them. King David is another painful example of a good leader who neglected his family. Tom Houston writes,

> The aggressive, passionate nature that David developed in his divided family made him one of the world's great kings but one of the world's worst fathers. He failed to counter the adverse effects of his family background as he created his own home, and he failed to order his home to avoid perpetuating the same adverse effects on the next generation. The cycle of trouble ran full circle and began again in the lives of his children.[25]

Finally, family should be a priority because **a strong family is the best validation of a leader's ministry.** A Christian leader, who loves and cares for his wife and raises happy and obedient children,

---

[25]Tom Houston, *King David* (n.p.: MARC Europe, 1987), 149-150.

possesses a strong testimony of his credibility as a leader. A peaceful, well-managed home often speaks much more to business employees, work associates, or church members about God's character than any Bible verses you might share with them. Certainly, this is what Paul meant when he said that marriage should reflect the relationship of Christ and the church (Ephesians 5:21-33). Your marriage and home provides a living testimony of the Gospel to which you testify.

When I said my wedding vows to my wife, I made a promise to her that, with God's help, I would not place my ministry above our personal relationship. I did that because I had the priorities mentioned above. I do not always successfully keep these priorities straight, but that is my goal. I have set my relationships in that order because I believe it is God's desire for me and for you. Examine your priorities. Have you allowed your work or ministry to come before family? If so, let's look at how you can change.

Making family a priority

When a leader realizes that God wants him to make his family a priority, then he can begin to make changes that will dramatically strengthen his family relationships. Making family a priority is summarized in one word, TIME.

You cannot say that your family is number one if you do not spend time with them. The way you spend your time will tell me more about your priorities than anything that you might say about your family.

The tendency of many Christian leaders is to give more time to work than to their families, expecting that their families will understand the importance of what they are doing. But building a strong family takes time; God does not provide special shortcuts or exceptions for busy leaders. Giving time to your family will take a lot of discipline and a

> Making family a priority is summarized in one word, TIME!

strong resolve but it can and must be done. You should set aside meaningful time with your family in at least three different areas.

Time with your spouse

Any growing relationship takes time and marriage is no exception. A leader can easily allow the busyness of life to keep him apart from the one person that God has given him as a partner in life. Slowly and silently a husband and wife begin to drift apart emotionally, intellectually and spiritually. Only a conscious effort to spend time together will counteract this natural tendency.

You must be intentional about spending time alone with your spouse. This means quality time, when you are both focused on the other and seeking to build your relationship, not just time together in the same room watching television or checking email. An article in a major newspaper reported that the average couple married ten years or more spends only thirty-seven minutes a week in meaningful communication.[26] That is not nearly enough time to build and maintain a strong relationship.

Eugene Habecker makes a strong statement we would do well to read frequently.

> Many leaders have an idolatrous relationship with another "mistress" called "the ministry" that demands long hours, time away from home, and is used to justify all kinds of unbiblical priorities. This kind of idolatry must be labeled for what it is - sin. The illicit affairs with the corporate mistress have got to stop. God's priorities cannot be ignored. He expects leaders to love their spouses as He loved the church. And this requires that the leader not neglect the needs - all of them - of the spouse.[27]

Talk to your spouse about how you can improve the time you spend together. You may be able to put the children to bed early enough to have some uninterrupted time every evening before bed. Take time to share your experiences and feelings and to pray together.

---

[26]John C. Maxwell, *The Success Journey* (Nashville, TN.: Nelson Business, 1997), 175.
[27]Habecker, *Rediscovering the Soul of Leadership*, 49.

Discuss your family plans and goals, the progress of the children and many other important family issues. Wives often long for this and wait for their husband to provide it for them. Men need to take responsibility, even when it does not come naturally, and learn to show love to their wives in this way.

Gary Smalley, a family expert, challenges men with these words, "If a couple has been married for more than five years, any persistent disharmony in their marriage is usually attributable to the husband's lack of understanding and applying genuine love."[28]

T. Engstrom and E. Dayton provide another reminder for leaders:

> God's work will get done without you. God is really not nervous about the future. Isn't He much more concerned with what you are than with what you accomplish, and isn't what you are demonstrated by the relationships you have? And isn't the most profound of those relationships the one you have with your wife? Have you left your wife? We pray she will take you back.[29]

Plan how you will spend time with your wife. If you have not been doing it at all, start with three times a week and then move towards sharing together every day. The improvement in your marriage will be worth the effort.

Time with your children

God intends children to grow up in a loving, caring environment. He gives parents the responsibility of training their children for 18 or more years until they are ready to become adults. This major responsibility calls for a significant time investment.

Take time to learn to know your children as individuals. They each have different temperaments and unique gifts. They see life from different perspectives. They need encouragement when they fail; they need affirmation to build their self-identity; they need loving

---

[28] Gary Smalley, *If Only He Knew* (Grand Rapids, MI.: Zondervan, 1982).
[29] Qtd. in Habecker, *Rediscovering the Soul of Leadership*, 51.

discipline when they err; they need a tender touch to feel loved; and they need to know their parents value them. All of this takes time.

Seize the moments when you come home from work. Ask questions about their day and really listen when they talk. Pursue times alone with each of your children. Go for a short walk or have a soda together. Take each of them out for lunch on a rotating basis. They will cherish the attention much more than the food.

Time together as a family

Individual times with your spouse and with individual children are essential but you also need to plan times together as a family, in order to develop the sense of belonging and identity that is a part of God's plan for the family. Plan for two types of time together; time to learn and time to laugh.

1. Time for learning

God gives parents, especially fathers, the responsibility of teaching their children the Word of God. Ephesians 6:4 says, "Fathers, do not exasperate your children; instead, bring them up in the training and instruction of the Lord." Deuteronomy 11:18-19 also says,

> Fix these words of mine in your hearts and minds; tie them as symbols on your hands and bind them on your foreheads. Teach them to your children, talking about them when you sit at home and when you walk along the road, when you lie down and when you get up.

This responsibility cannot be delegated to the Sunday school teacher.

Biblical instruction can happen in many ways, but I suggest that you plan a daily time for your family to share the Word of God and grow spiritually. This may be called "family devotions," "the family altar," "family worship," "Jesus time," or any other appropriate name. Whatever the name, it will change your home. This time can take various forms, but it will likely include Bible reading, prayer and singing together as a family. Here are some tips to help you begin a family devotional time.

• **Adjust to the ages of your children**

Make sure that your activities are geared toward the ages of your children; make Bible study interesting to them by keeping it at a level that they can understand. At an early age children can learn to enjoy this time together as a family, learning about and communicating with God. For young children you may have to tell the Bible story in very simple language with dramatic actions. Make it an adventure.

Avoid reading long passages to young children. If possible, buy a Bible storybook with pictures. Remember, that young children have short attention spans. If you pray with them for 20 minutes, they might be asleep when you say "Amen!" As they get older allow them to participate by reading or acting out the story.

Don't underestimate the ability of young children to grasp spiritual truths. Many times their faith will be a challenge to you. Learn to value their insights in spiritual issues.

• **Be creative**

Keep it interesting. Children need action. You don't want them to think that Jesus is boring simply because you cannot keep their attention. Think of different ways to tell the stories. Use drama. Sing different songs. As they get older, allow the children to lead or plan the time. What ever you do, do not do the same thing day after day. Be aware of your children's needs and struggles and focus on stories that address those needs, teaching them to value God's Word not just for its good stories, but also as a source of direction and comfort.

• **Be consistent**

Have family devotional time every day. Make it a part of your family routine, just before or after a meal, or at another time that suits your family best. Whether it is in the morning or in the evening, choose a time and then stick to it.

2. Time for fun

Not only do you need time with your family to teach them the word of God, but you also need time to have fun together. God enjoys celebrations and He made a wonderful world for us to enjoy together. Take advantage of holidays, birthdays and other special events to do fun things as a family, creating memories that will last a lifetime.

One way to have fun together is to designate a "family night" one night a week. These evenings are reserved just for you and your family and should include some sort of fun activity. Some ideas that my family has enjoyed have been a special meal, playing a game together, working together on a special project around the house and reading a book together.

Use your imagination. These evenings do not need to be expensive—they just need to provide an activity through which your family can interact positively and learn to enjoy each other. Eat with the special plates that you normally save for company, act out a drama, play a card game, take a walk, tell stories about your childhood or sing songs. Find out what sort of things each family member enjoys and try to incorporate all those elements, or allow your children to take turns choosing the activity.

When you start investing this kind of time in your family, beautiful things begin to happen. By showing your children that you value them and enjoy spending time with them, you are building strong leaders for the next generation. Confident in your love and approval, they will be quick to help and lead others, even from a young age. When you create a loving home atmosphere, your family relationships will give you the strength to minister to others and testify about the vibrancy of your Christian faith in the church and in the marketplace. This is your responsibility as a Christian leader. Take some time to complete the action assignment, which will help you make the needed changes in your family.

ACTION ASSIGNMENT

1. Reflect honestly on your family life. Does your family come before or after ministry on your priority list?

   Would your spouse agree with your answer? Why or why not?

2. If your priorities have been out of line with God's desire, take a few minutes in prayer asking God to forgive you and to change you.

3. Now that God has heard your repentance, you need to share your heart with your family. Schedule a time, today if possible, to sit with them and ask for their forgiveness. Put an "x" here when you have done this. _____

4. Make a plan of action for your family. You may do this in consultation with your spouse and children as appropriate. Be specific about what you will do and when you will do it for each of the areas below:

   Time with my spouse:

   Time with my children:

   Time with my family:

5. Make the above plan work. It will take a lot of commitment. You may need to say "no" to some other commitments that have previously taken away from your family time. Be serious with your schedule until your priorities are God's priorities. I pray that your family will become all that God wants it to be. God bless you as you lead at home!

Chapter Ten

THE LEADER AND TRANSITION
(Leaving Well)

Francis was angry. For the fifth time his evangelist's salary had been delayed. Pastor Solomon had not even apologized for the inconvenience. Francis felt like his long hours of work in the church were hardly recognized or appreciated. "Why should I keep working here?" he asked himself. "I think I would be better off starting my own church. I know the people I've been teaching are also unhappy with Pastor Solomon and there are enough of them to pay my salary. Anyway, I've always felt the call to serve God on my own."

For the next few months Francis thought about his options. He quietly shared his discouragement and frustration, as "prayer requests," with several people that he knew would be sympathetic. They gave him their support and began looking for an affordable meeting place. When Pastor Solomon left for a one-week trip to a neighboring country, Francis made his move. Twenty members of the old church joined him for the first Sunday service in the new location. Francis preached a powerful message on crossing over the Jordan into the Promised Land. He went home that evening feeling on top of the world. "At last, I'm free to do what God wants me to do," he whispered to his wife as he drifted off to sleep.

Francis' story is repeated almost daily in many different churches and situations, as dissatisfied leaders decide to move to a new location, denomination, church or ministry. It happens as well in the corporate world where workers and bosses leave their current positions for new ones. What does transition mean for a Christian leader? Is there a right and wrong way to leave? How can you know the proper time to leave? What are some of the pitfalls of leaving that you need to avoid? This chapter is dedicated to answering these questions.

Principles Of Leaving Well

Let's examine three foundational principles about leaving.

Principle One: Leaving is sometimes an inevitable part of growth

Although many people tend to view leaving negatively, it is not always wrong; sometimes it is an inevitable part of growth. Leaders have different personalities, different visions, and different goals that often push people in different directions. This is one way that God often launches two separate organizations, both of which will accomplish great things for His kingdom.

At other times, leaving is simply sinful pride and rebellion that creates division among God's people and wounds the people involved. Even in rebellious situations, however, God's grace can use the division for the multiplication of His work. An example of this is the separation of Barnabas and Paul in Acts 15. They had a disagreement that caused them to split, resulting in two ministry teams going out in different directions.

Sometimes two or more people begin working together because they need each other's abilities. As they each grow in their leadership ability, however, they find their need for each other lessening and the friction between them increasing. If they separate in a healthy manner, with no hard feelings, it can be a good sign of growth for both parties. People often ask if denominations are good. Nearly every denomination began as a split from an existing group, and although I do not think God planned for His church to be so divided, He does use denominations for His glory.

Often God uses different denominations to reflect different aspects of His own nature in a way that no single group could. At times denominations lose their original vision and a group breaks off that is open to a fresh move of God. Again, if this is done in the right manner, it can be a healthy part of church growth and expansion.

Sometimes transition is simply a part of God's plan for your life. He wanted you to be in one place or ministry for a certain time and then He calls you to move on. This happened to me after I was a pastor for six years and then received a call to a ministry working with leaders. It had nothing to do with division or disagreements; it was simply God's next step for my family and it was time for me to move to something new. Career changes have become a routine part of modern life in the corporate world and are often a sign of individual or organizational growth.

Principle Two: Leaving should be done with integrity

When God wants a separation to take place, He has a method that will bring the best results. Often, in the haste of departure or the emotion of the moment, people forget some crucial principles and take short cuts in order to reach their desired end more quickly. The goal should be to leave with integrity, to be able to say at the end, "I left in a manner that was consistent with God's nature and biblical principles." The one leaving should do his best to make this happen. This chapter is devoted to learning how to leave with integrity.

Principle Three: The manner of leaving determines the outcome of the transition

If leaving is done in a manner consistent with Biblical principles it should yield a positive outcome. When God's principles are violated, the result will be less than desirable. The spirit and attitude of the person leaving are often the determining factors in whether the outcome is positive or negative.

I have seen many people leave churches with good reasons and good intentions. But the manner in which they left deposited seeds of rebellion and discord in their own ministries that later yielded bad fruit. In a similar way I have observed both healthy and unhealthy professional transitions.

The Process Of Leaving

In looking at the process of leaving, it is helpful to break apart the word "LEAVE" and allow each letter to stand for one part of the process for Christian leaders:

Look at your motives
Examine your responsibility
Ask for blessing
Value relationships
Exit completely

Look at your motives

Before taking the step of leaving, take a close look at your motives. What is the real reason that you want to leave? Be careful that you do not allow your heart to deceive you. The Bible says, "The heart is deceitful above all things and beyond cure. Who can understand it?" (Jeremiah 17:9). Dig below your surface explanations to discover your foundational reason for leaving. Do any of these common reasons explain your situation?

- A personality conflict
- A desire for more money
- A difference in vision
- A different calling/gifting
- A desire to move "up" in position
- A desire to be independent
- A wish to be the person in charge

Be specific and face the foundational issue squarely in your heart. Pray about the issue, asking God to search your heart and to purify your motives. Not all the motives listed are necessarily wrong but it is crucial to be consciously aware of why you want to move. You can always convince other people that your actions are justified, but God is the final judge. You will answer to Him for your decision to move.

Also, seek godly counsel from people who know you well and will challenge you deeply regarding your motives. Whether or not you are able to receive and consider their counsel often serves as an indicator of your heart motives. If your move places you in a higher position than you previously held, do you plan to submit yourself to another authority? Many people leave because they are tired of being under authority. God will not bless that kind of move.

> Many people leave because they are tired of being under authority.

When I left the pastoral ministry I examined my motives. Did I simply desire a change or was God really calling me elsewhere? I discussed the matter with my wife and sought counsel from people in authority over me. Together we sensed God's clear direction. Their counsel held me accountable and their affirmation provided the confirmation that I was moving forward with pure motives.

Examine your responsibility

When you leave because of a difference of opinion or vision, you must first examine your part in that disagreement. Instead of focusing on how others have wronged or misunderstood you, look at the ways that you have been responsible for the conflict. Although it is much easier to see the other person's fault, very rarely is one party 100 percent at fault. Have you consistently shown respect and loyalty to those in authority over you? In what ways did you contribute to the difference of opinion? When dealing with the issue, did you always respond in the Spirit of Christ? Have you done all that you can to resolve the difference? If you do not adequately resolve these issues you will carry them with you to the new assignment.

Ask for blessing

God releases blessing and anointing for ministry through authority figures. A leader, therefore, needs the blessing of an authority in order to be commissioned into ministry. (See the more detailed discussion of this in Chapter Seven.) When God calls you to a different place, you should go with the blessing of your authority.

Sometimes the authority will refuse to give their blessing, but leaving with integrity demands that you do all that you can to receive a blessing from your authority before you part ways. It is always wrong to sneak away and start a new church or ministry without revealing your plans to your colleague(s) and endeavoring to resolve any conflicts or misunderstandings.

You should be as open as possible with your leader(s), even when you feel wronged or misunderstood. Such vulnerability may seem risky but it indicates pure motives and a clean heart. Receiving a blessing involves sharing your heart with your leader(s), being open about your desires and intentions. Secrecy and distrust only undermines your credibility and plants those same seeds into your new ministry.

Jacob's departure from Laban's house provides a biblical example of this principle. Jacob secretly fled, fearing that Laban would not release him. When Laban caught up with him he said,

> Why did you run off secretly and deceive me? Why didn't you tell me, so that I could send you away with joy and singing to the music of tambourines and harps? You didn't even let me kiss my grandchildren and my daughters good-bye. You have done a foolish thing (Genesis 31:27-28).

Laban goes on to say that he could have harmed Jacob for leaving secretly, except that the Lord told him in a dream to leave Jacob alone. He saw Jacob's leaving without his blessing as equal to stealing. Later, because of God's intervention, Laban and Jacob make a covenant not to harm each other and Laban gives a blessing to his daughters and grandchildren.

When the authority over you is unwilling to bless you, make very sure that you are obeying God's direction (and not just your own inclinations) before taking any action. As discussed in Chapter Seven, God often speaks through authority figures. Perhaps your authority sees some rough edges in your character that need to be shaped. He may sense a negative attitude in you that God still wants to remove. He may even be the vehicle that God wants to use to remove that negative attitude from your heart.

David waited many years to become king, although he knew that he was called and that King Saul was unfit for office. He learned many lessons that shaped his character as he waited for God's timing to lead. Let that example give you a lot of caution about leaving without a blessing. When leaving a job or position in an organization, make certain that you do your best not only to comply with notification requirements, but seek the best way to work with those in authority to enable a smooth transition.

When blessing is withheld, you should seek God about timing. Perhaps the direction is correct but it is not yet the right time for the change. In my transition, I needed to give the church leadership time to think and pray about my moving before they could bless me. In the end, they were ready to bless my family and me in our next step and we left with relationships intact and an open door for further interaction.

Value relationships
Leaving with integrity requires that you value relationships with all your brothers and sisters in Christ. Paul writes, "If it is possible, as far as it depends on you, live at peace with everyone" (Romans 12:18).

Often relationships become tense during the leaving process. Both sides focus on the negative aspects of the other. Francis could no longer recognize Pastor Solomon's good qualities. He forgot that Pastor Solomon led him to the Lord and discipled him as a young believer. Employees often forget what they have gained professionally or relationally from their time with the organization they are now leaving.

No matter how painful a relationship becomes, you must make an effort to remember and be thankful for the positive aspects, both past and present, of that relationship. Remember too that relationships are valuable. In the future you may again need the advice, support or encouragement of the person with whom you are now disagreeing. Leave as friends.

Valuing relationships means placing a careful guard over your lips. In the heat of a disagreement it is easy to say more than you should about the other person and the nature of your disagreement. You may want to gain sympathy or a following, or even to justify your actions, but you must resist this temptation at all costs. When you leave because of a disagreement, all that you need to say is, "I differed with the leader on several issues and we agreed to separate." You do not need to give all the details.

Exit completely

When the time to leave comes, you must exit completely. Many leaders want to leave their former position while continuing to carry the relationships, property or privileges that they gained there. Exiting completely involves several things.

First, you must be willing to leave behind all that does not belong to you, including any **relationships** that you developed while under someone else's leadership. If you served as an associate pastor or evangelist, you were building the ministry of your leader. Now that you are leaving, you must be willing to relinquish relational connections. Do not pursue people that you used to visit in your old position. Do not try to take them with you. They are not your people. If you plow someone else's field as their worker, when you decide to leave their employment you cannot collect the grain in the field. The harvest belongs to the owner. Businesses often have legally binding agreements to enforce this principle, but Christian leaders should do it willingly and follow not only the letter but the spirit of the law.

Sometimes this means that Christian leaders should **physically move** away from the region of your former position. Many church leaders are not willing to pay this price and they end up moving only a short distance away and taking some of the members from the former church. While this may look and feel good at the present time, be aware that you are planting a seed for the same sort of rebellion to happen to you in the future of your new ministry. If any members of your former church want to follow you, require them to talk with their pastor and ask for his blessing before you accept them as your members.

When I took a new position after a pastoral role, my wife and I decided that we should move away from the community where we had been pastoring a church. Leaving the relationships that had been so much a part of our lives for six years was painful, but we realized that we were no longer the leadership team and that we needed to make a clear break with those relationships. It would be unfair to the new pastor if we left the responsibilities of leading the people, but still maintained the privileges of their affection.

Finally, you should also leave behind the **physical property** of your former employer, including records, files, letters, office equipment, keys and any other official items. These items belong to the position you held, not to you individually. Make sure, also, to give a full report to your superior of all finished and unfinished matters that were under your attention. This will facilitate a smoother transition for the person who will fill your position. If you are truly leaving in the spirit of Christ, without bitterness, you will want to bless the organization instead of making the transition logistically difficult.

When these principles and procedures are followed, leaving does not have to be a painful and frustrating experience. When it is God's time for you to leave, do it in God's way and transition can be a time of growth for you and the organization you leave as well as the one you join. I love Luke's simple description of one of Paul's many transitions, "But when our time was up, we left and continued on our way" (Acts 21:5). Let's follow his example.

ACTION ASSIGNMENT

1. Reflect on any transitions you have made up to this point in your life. Were they done in a healthy manner?

   If not, what do you need to do to make it right?

2. Look ahead to the future. If you ever feel God calling you to a change in ministry, will you commit yourself to follow the steps outlined in this chapter? Take a moment in prayer and ask God to give you the courage to do so.

3. Take this chapter to your boss/superior and ask him to read it and then discuss together how you can make a healthy transition if the need arises. Commit yourself to be open and honest with him/her. Put an "x" here when you have done this. _____

Chapter Eleven

THE LEADER AND ENDURANCE
(Finishing Well)

"I have fought the good fight, I have finished the race, I have kept the faith. Now there is in store for me the crown of righteousness, which the Lord, the righteous Judge, will award to me on that day - and not only to me, but also to all who have longed for His appearing" (2 Timothy 4:7-8).

Beginning well in leadership is not enough. You may be a great "success" in your twenties, thirties or forties, but you are not truly successful unless you finish well in your later years. And the only way to finish well is to run well.

Many leaders began with a sincere desire to serve God. They were humble, being small in their own eyes. They felt inadequate for the task and spent much time praying and fasting. God came to them with His anointing; empowered them with His Holy Spirit; and prospered their labor. As they prospered in ministry, a slow and subtle change occurred, and the anointing of God was lifted.

173

This can easily happen to any man or woman. Let's try to understand from Scripture how it happens, and how you can prevent it in your own life and leadership. We'll look at two leaders from the scripture, King Uzziah and King Solomon.

King Uzziah (2 Chronicles 26)

Pick up your Bible and read the story of King Uzziah. This section focuses on several key verses, but reading the whole chapter will give you a better perspective on his story. After you've finished reading, let's look at several things from his life. 2 Chronicles 26:3-5 says,

> Uzziah was sixteen years old when he became king, and he reigned in Jerusalem for fifty-two years. His mother's name was Jecoliah; she was from Jerusalem. He did what was right in the eyes of the LORD, just as his father Amaziah had done. He sought God during the days of Zechariah, who instructed him in the fear of God. As long as he sought the LORD, God gave him success.

Several significant points emerge from this account. Uzziah was young, godly, humble and teachable, so God prospered him, and he succeeded as king.

In verses 6-15 we see that he defeated his enemies, he built cities, he received tribute from others, he became famous and he acquired great strength. He built towers in many places, prospered in agriculture and assembled a large and well-equipped army. He stood as a model of a successful king, a man of God whose life was marked by God's favor.

But reread the last phrase of verse 15, "for he was greatly helped *until* he became powerful" (emphasis added). All went well until he was strong.

Verse 16 explains what happened next. "But after Uzziah became powerful, his pride led to his downfall. He was unfaithful to the LORD his God, and entered the temple of the LORD to burn incense on the altar of incense." When the priests challenged Uzziah (17-18) he became enraged (19), believing that as king he could do anything he wanted.

This great king, wonderfully blessed by God and marked by His presence, was struck with leprosy and cut off from the house of God. He began well but finished tragically. Though his life contained many successes, he ultimately failed because he did not have the character to finish well.

King Solomon (1 Kings 3:1 to 11:14)

King Solomon provides another example of a leader who began very well but finished terribly. We read in 1 Kings 3:3 that "Solomon showed his love for the LORD by walking according to the statutes of his father David." He pleased God so much that God appeared to him in a dream and said, "Ask for whatever you want Me to give you" (3:5).

This was Solomon's chance – the opportunity for divine blessing in a proportion of which other leaders can only dream. He could ask for riches, fame, power or anything he wanted with the full assurance of God's blessing. Instead, he asked for wisdom. He said, "So give Your servant a discerning heart to govern Your people and to distinguish between right and wrong. For who is able to govern this great people of Yours?" (3:9)

What about Solomon moved him to make such a request? In 1 Kings 3:7-8 Solomon confessed that he felt like a little child and expressed his personal inability to do the work of God. He acknowledged his position as God's servant and spoke of the people as "Your people." Solomon's heart was tender and humble before God and his concern was for his responsibility to God's people.

And God honored his request, "I will do what you have asked. I will give you a wise and discerning heart, so that there will never have been anyone like you, nor will there ever be" (3:12). Not only would Solomon be the wisest man to ever live, but God also gave him everything else that he might have asked for (3:13-14). These blessings came, however, with a condition: "*if* you walk in My ways and obey My statutes" (3:14).

God's continued blessing was dependent upon Solomon's continued obedience. This principle applies to all leaders. Many have risen to a certain level because of God's blessing. Impressed by their success, however, they become proud and begin to disobey God's commands. They continue to minister in God's name, but God has removed his blessing and power from them because of their disobedience.

You and I have never known a man that God prospered to the degree that He prospered Solomon. Read 1 Kings 3:28-10:25. The level of God's favor is beyond comprehension. Read also Ecclesiastes 2:4-10. Clearly Solomon was a mighty man of God. If he were a contemporary business leader he would be the CEO of a multinational corporation. If he were a 21st Century pastor, he would lead a mega-church movement.

But then Solomon's story changes drastically. This great man of God crashes from his glorious height. In order to understand what happens next, you must look at Deuteronomy 17:14-20 where God gives instructions to Israel's future kings. In these verses God lists three things that the kings were forbidden to do:

> The king, moreover, must not *acquire great numbers of horses* for himself or make the people return to Egypt to get more of them, for the LORD has told you, "You are not to go back that way again." He must not *take many wives*, or his heart will be led astray. He must not *accumulate large amounts of silver and gold* (Deuteronomy 17:16-17, italics mine).

God clearly instructed the king not to acquire many horses from Egypt, which would symbolize a dependence on military might instead of God's protection. He also commanded the king not to take many wives, who would lead his heart astray and convince him to serve their gods. Finally, God warned the king not to acquire large amounts of silver and gold, which could lead him to abuse his power and rely on material wealth instead of God for provision.

In verses 18-19, God orders the king to keep the Scriptures prominent in his life, and in verse 20 He gives both a warning and a promise: the king should "not consider himself better than his brothers and turn from the law to the right or to the left. Then he and his descendants will reign a long time over his kingdom in Israel."

With this background we can now look at what happened to King Solomon. **Read 1 Kings 10:23-11:14.** Solomon's trouble began when he chose to disregard the clear instruction of God. In 10:23 we read, "King Solomon was greater in riches and wisdom than all the other kings of the earth." We learn in 10:28 that he imported horses from Egypt. And finally, in 11:1-8, we learn he "loved many foreign women." All three actions were in direct disobedience to God's instruction in Deuteronomy. Solomon enjoyed these things for a while, but ultimately they led to a tragic ending to his reign as king.

> How could one so clearly marked by God, fail so horribly?

How could the one who wrote, "The fear of the LORD is the beginning of knowledge, but fools despise wisdom and discipline" (Proverbs 1:7), do such a foolish thing? How could one so clearly marked by God, fail so horribly? Hadn't God written His approval across Solomon's life in permanent ink?

The reason men fall

God intends every good thing that He gives to you to be dedicated to Him and used for His purposes. This includes intelligence, education, wisdom, humility, public speaking gifts, material things, the ministry gifts listed in Scripture and every other good thing you possess. God entrusts them to you so that He may use them to accomplish His work on earth. Their use brings glory to Him, life to the people you know and joy to you.

Satan, however, is desperate to hinder God's glorious purposes. He is untiring in his attempts to spoil and distort the good gifts of God, turning them into something that serves his sinful purposes. Although you as a Christian are not under his authority, Satan knows that he can often deceive you through the pride of the human heart.

The Apostle Paul speaks of Satan's plan when he writes,

> To keep me from becoming conceited because of these surpassingly great revelations, there was given me a thorn in my flesh, a messenger of Satan, to torment me. Three times I pleaded with the Lord to take it away from me. But he said to me, "My grace is sufficient for you, for my power is made perfect in weakness." Therefore I will boast all the more gladly about my weaknesses, so that Christ's power may rest on me. That is why, for Christ's sake, I delight in weaknesses, in insults, in hardships, in persecutions, in difficulties. For when I am weak, then I am strong (2 Corinthians 12:7-10).

Paul knew that his success could easily become the root of failure. People often believe that the higher a man rises in leadership, the stronger he becomes spiritually. They honor him and sometimes envy him for his apparent stature.

Although it is never directly stated as such, people often imagine their leader to be above the standards of normal humanity. In their minds he becomes almost invincible – so close to God that he is above the temptations of ordinary men. It is easy to believe near perfection of men who appear successful; and those men are prone to believe the same about themselves.

> The more successful you become in God's kingdom, the more alert you must be to Satan's temptations.

For this reason, the more successful you become, the more alert you must be to Satan's temptations. He will weave his lies into your blessings like a cancer that becomes entwined around body organs. He will speak lies about your leadership and character that seem good, but which, if you believe them, will form the foundation of your failure.

For example, as a strong leader, you may be tempted to control those around you rather then equipping, empowering and releasing them. Satan will tell you that you must control your followers, who are clearly less mature and often lack discernment, so that you can protect and preserve what God has done for His further use and glory. But control is not part of God's heart or character. Satan uses this lie, which seems to serve a godly end, to appeal to the true motives of your heart – to protect what God has done in a way that will maintain your position and importance.

Satan uses several common tactics to lead men astray, so that the glory of God will be lifted from their lives.

Self-realization and pride

As your leadership gift grows, it will touch many people who will affirm your position and abilities. The more others praise you, the more you will begin to define yourself in light of your leadership gifts. They become a conscious part of how you relate to others, and often you begin to feel and act superior. Pride begins to sneak into your heart and mind. Slowly, you begin to think and act as though the good things that happen through you are actually the result of your skills and power. You believe that you are the gift, instead of simply being a vessel that contains the gift.

Others congratulate you, saying, "That was a wonderful message" or "Your ability in sales is outstanding" and you start to define yourself as "the preacher" or "the salesman of the month." You easily forget that God, working through the gift that He placed within you, is the one who is actually producing the fruit. You fail to realize that the only gift that is useful to God is the one exercised in humility, the one that proclaims God's glory and not the vessel's. How much success do you need before you will be tempted with pride? Very little.

Every blessing can potentially distance you from God. Every gift that He gives to enrich your life and leadership can lead to self-sufficiency and pride, moving you away from His purposes and toward self-fulfillment.

Before I move ahead, allow me to add a word of caution concerning pride. You must be discerning when considering whether you are proud. I have seen humble, godly men who were restrained in their leadership because they believed a voice in their heads, telling them they were proud. They thought this voice was the Holy Spirit. Because they knew that pride is wrong, they confessed it as sin and asked God's forgiveness. Still, the voice persisted. Flooded by guilt, they pulled back from joyfully exercising the gift that God gave them.

I am convinced that Satan uses genuine pride to pull down many Christian leaders. I am just as convinced that if Satan tempts a man with pride and the man refuses it, that Satan will attack at the back door and try to convince him that his enjoyment of the gift that God gave him is pride. He may whisper, "You shouldn't feel good when you do that; you must be proud." But the truth is that you should enjoy doing what God created you to do.

Finding joy and satisfaction in your calling is not wrong. You should diligently resist the enemy's attempts to make you feel guilty for what is not pride. He is crafty. He will do anything that he can to intimidate you and keep you from using God's good gifts. You must learn to discern between true pride and false accusation; receiving the Holy Spirit's voice but refusing Satan's. Satan's voice is filled with condemnation and despair while the Holy Spirit's voice brings hope.

The distraction of success

As your labor prospers under God's anointing, your organization will grow and you may be frequently

> Success is often a root of failure.

sought after as a guest speaker. People may begin to flock to hear you, and you will naturally be excited by the admiration in the eyes and voices.

Slowly, things change. You may begin to think of yourself as a big man, becoming great in your own eyes. Tight schedules, meetings with important people and eating good food gradually begin to replace prayer and fasting. Power increasingly shapes your ministry.

You become caught up with maintaining your image and find less and less time for seeking the heart of God and ministering to the needs of people. Though you formerly trusted God for your daily needs, you now spend much of your time trying to generate enough income to maintain the lifestyle you have come to expect for yourself and your family. Success has the power to slowly draw you away from dependence on God and in this way is often a root of failure.

Forgetting God

In Deuteronomy 8:10-18 God warned Israel of the danger of forgetting Him.

> When you have eaten and are satisfied, praise the LORD your God for the good land he has given you. Be careful that you do not forget the LORD your God, failing to observe his commands, his laws and his decrees that I am giving you this day. Otherwise, when you eat and are satisfied, when you build fine houses and settle down, and when your herds and flocks grow large and your silver and gold increase and all you have is multiplied, then your heart will become proud and you will forget the LORD your God, who brought you out of Egypt, out of the land of slavery. He led you through the vast and dreadful desert, that thirsty and waterless land, with its venomous snakes and scorpions. He brought you water out of hard rock. He gave you manna to eat in the desert, something your fathers had never known, to humble and to test you so that in the end it might go well with you. You may say to yourself, "My power and the strength of my hands have

produced this wealth for me." But remember the LORD your God, for it is he who gives you the ability to produce wealth, and so confirms his covenant, which he swore to your forefathers, as it is today.

God recognized the danger of success. He warned His people that prosperity would come after their struggles and that with prosperity came the danger of forgetting the God who provided for them.

Every servant of God will be tempted to forget God when he experiences success – even the success that comes through the blessing of God. You must remember that it is God who has empowered you and brought you success.

Writing your own rules

One of the subtle temptations of success is to think that you ought to be able to write your own rules. At a certain level of success, you may easily begin to think that you are above the laws that others need to obey.

King Uzziah certainly knew that he was not allowed to offer incense on the altar. He did not sin because of a lack of knowledge. Rather, he arrogantly believed himself above the law and able do things that others could not. He thought himself capable of modifying the rules to suit his own desires. And when confronted, he defended himself.

King Solomon's story follows the same pattern. He knew he was breaking the rules when he accumulated riches, imported horses from Egypt and took many wives. But he could justify his actions. Perhaps he thought he deserved a few pleasures after all he had done for God. Or maybe he assumed that God's clear blessing and approval gave him some liberty with the rules. After all, it was the power that God gave him that enabled his choices.

Many leaders do this today. After reaching a measure of success, they begin doing things that they never would have accepted in earlier years. They write new rules in areas like morality, accumulation of wealth, lifestyle, courtesy in driving, the disciplines of prayer and fasting, expense accounts and much more.

It is easy to convince yourself that faithful service to God entitles you to a few exceptions. You may even begin to believe that the letter of the law was designed for less mature leaders. In the world, privilege accompanies power, and as a successful and influential Christian leader, you want to believe that God permits your compromise in a few areas. Many leaders have stumbled on this point.

Unfortunately, followers often encourage such behavior. Followers like big people. They enjoy some extravagant displays of wealth: of the rich lifestyle, the fancy vehicles and the advanced electronics. Perhaps this is because the followers hope that some day they might become big themselves. Or maybe they know they will never have such a lavish lifestyle, but feel better about themselves through being a part of the life of someone who does.

When you start accepting in your own life what you would never allow in someone else's, you are beginning to walk the slippery road of self-deception.

Finding your identity in leadership

All leaders are tempted to find identity, security and worth in what they do. What you do can quickly become more important than who you are. You discard your identity as a child of God and find your identity as a preacher, teacher, businessman, lawyer, etc. When this happens, your tendency will be to quickly try to make your work bigger and better since this will make you bigger and better as a person.

When your identity is found in your leadership several problems can emerge.

1. You are very professional at work or "spiritual" at church but much less so when at home.
2. You fail to minister sufficiently to your family. Your dissatisfied wife and rebellious children disqualify you from leadership.
3. You may become a controlling leader, trying to protect your position so that you can continue to feel good about yourself.

4. You may stay in a position where you are comfortable, instead of moving into the new work that God prepared for you.

Every leader will face this temptation. But you must find your wholeness, importance and sense of well being in your relationship with God and not in the work that you perform for Him. You are His son or daughter, loved by Him and complete as a human being on that basis alone. If you are faithful with the gift He has entrusted to you, you are just as important to Him, whether you do little or much; whether you appear to be big or small in the world.

The sin that follows

In 1 Timothy 5:24-25, Paul says, "The sins of some men are obvious, reaching the place of judgment ahead of them; the sins of others trail behind them. In the same way, good deeds are obvious, and even those that are not cannot be hidden."

There are men whose sins are seen immediately. These sins might include immorality, drunkenness or serious character flaws. But others are able to hide their sins for a long time. They might have a serious problem with greed, inferiority or sexuality but are able to keep it from being evident in their actions. But, when burnout hits and their defenses are weakened, or when they become successful in leadership and believe they can write their own rules, they will begin to openly practice the sin that has been hidden in their hearts.

Many have witnessed the fall of true servants of God who failed to deal with their own potentially destructive weaknesses. Take warning. Deal with the "small" sins now, before success in leadership opens a door for the devil to reveal those areas of your life. Build a solid foundation that will enable you to finish well.

When you give in to Satan's trap in any of these areas, God's blessing will be removed from your life and leadership. If you realize that the power has left, you may be tempted to continue leading in your own strength. When you do that, you lower your leadership from divine to human and it loses its glory. The harder you try, the farther you will move from the true gift and the more superficial you will become.

In leadership, this will lead to manipulation and excessive exercise of authority. In the church it may result in a cult, false prophecy or counterfeit gifts of healing and miracles. In other settings it leads to dictatorial rather than servant leadership.

Keys To Finish Well

No one plans to finish poorly but most leaders have never thought deeply about what it will take for them to finish well. Here are several principles to help you to finish well.

Remain small in your own eyes
Note that both Uzziah and Solomon were small in their own eyes when they began. They lived with humility and a teachable spirit until they became powerful.

In 2 Corinthians 12:7-10 Paul accepted a thorn in the flesh because it made him feel weaker. He teaches that when he felt weak in himself, that then he was actually strong in Christ.

Remaining small in your own eyes is difficult when God blesses your leadership. Keep reminding yourself constantly that it is God's work, for His glory, and that only His blessing causes the work to prosper.

Have a clear goal in your life
The Apostle Paul knew his potential for failure at the end of his career. In 1 Corinthians 9:24-27 he calls believers to "Run in such a way as to get the prize." He speaks of self-control and of having a clear goal for your life. He said, "I beat my body and make it my slave so that after I have preached to others, I myself will not be disqualified for the prize" (1 Corinthians 9:27). Paul constantly focused on a clear goal for his life because he wanted to finish well.

His goal – to not be disqualified – gave him direction and shaped his response to both deep trials and great successes. He adds in his letter to the church at Philippi:

> I want to know Christ and the power of his resurrection and the fellowship of sharing in his sufferings, becoming like him in his death, and so, somehow, to attain to the resurrection from the dead. Not that I have already obtained all this, or have already been made perfect, but I press on to take hold of that for which Christ Jesus took hold of me. Brothers, I do not consider myself yet to have taken hold of it. But one thing I do: Forgetting what is behind and straining towards what is ahead, I press on towards the goal to win the prize for which God has called me heavenwards in Christ Jesus (3:10-14).

These verses reveal Paul's humility and his deep desire to persevere towards his goal. Paul did not focus simply on opening churches or making a name for himself, he set the heavenly prize as his goal.

Earthly things did not bring satisfaction or a sense of success to Paul. Satisfaction and success came only through knowing Christ, through being connected to God's work in the world and through embracing an eternal, heaven-bound perspective. He consciously sought after the Kingdom that made even the greatest riches and honors of this world seem pale and insignificant in comparison. He had a higher goal. If only Uzziah and Solomon had taken the same approach.

Keep God's Word

In Deuteronomy 17:18-20, God established a command for all future kings:

> When he takes the throne of his kingdom, he is to write for himself on a scroll a copy of this law, taken from that of the priests, who are Levites. It is to be with him, and he is to read it all the days of his life so that he may learn to

revere the LORD his God and follow carefully all the words of this law and these decrees and not consider himself better than his brothers and turn from the law to the right or to the left. Then he and his descendants will reign a long time over his kingdom in Israel.

These words should significantly impact leaders today. You must keep God's Word in a prominent place in your heart and life if you expect to be a godly and effective leader.

As soon as busyness in leadership usurps your time in God's Word, you are in trouble. You need God's Word to challenge and rebuke you, to hold you accountable and remind you of the central truths of the gospel. Without daily rebukes and reminders from God's Word, you cannot effectively serve Him or the people you lead.

> As soon as busyness in ministry usurps your time in God's Word, you are in trouble.

Deal with hidden sins

You may find it easy to allow hidden sins to remain in your life. But if you want to finish well, you must decide early in your career to deal with the hidden sins in your life. If you do not establish this commitment, as your leadership grows, you will become increasingly able to justify your sin. Paul shows us the right way when he says, "we have renounced secret and shameful ways" (2 Corinthians 4:2). Remember that your sins will come to the surface in time. Take a moment now and ask God to search your heart for the hidden sins that you have allowed to remain in your life. Repent and seek His cleansing from them.

Keep your perspective

If you want to finish well, you must maintain a proper perspective on God's purposes for blessing and prospering you. According to 1

Peter 2:9-10, you are part of a chosen race and a royal priesthood, so that you can make Him known to others. In Jeremiah 33:6-9, God reveals the ultimate purpose for His blessing:

> Nevertheless, I will bring health and healing to it; I will heal my people and will let them enjoy abundant peace and security. I will bring Judah and Israel back from captivity and will rebuild them as they were before. I will cleanse them from all the sin they have committed against me and will forgive all their sins of rebellion against me.
>
> *Then this city will bring me renown, joy, praise and honor before all nations on earth that hear of all the good things I do for it; and they will be in awe and will tremble at the abundant prosperity and peace I provide for it.* (emphasis added)

God's blessing serves one purpose – to bring *Him* honor and praise. This is His desire for all churches, all businesses, and all other organizations.

Not only do you need to remember why God blesses you, also keep a proper perspective on what God does through you. Remember, His power alone changes lives. He does not need your teaching skills, your persuasive oratory, your anointed hands or your gifted administration to change people's lives. Only the Holy Spirit performs those wonders for God.

God, in His infinite grace, allows you to take part in His work, not because He needs you, but because He loves you and rejoices at your service. Zechariah 4:6 serves as a needed reminder: "Not by might nor by power, but by my Spirit, says the LORD Almighty." Memorize this verse as a reminder to keep you humble the next time that God uses you for something great.

Recognize your vulnerability

If you want to finish well, you must recognize your own vulnerability and susceptibility to the temptations that Uzziah and Solomon faced. All leaders face temptations that increase in proportion to the success of your work. The sad reality is that many leaders do not finish well, as many as two-thirds of Biblical leaders did not finish well.[30] This is a sober warning. If you fail to diligently guard your humility before God, you too will not finish well. The only safeguard against Satan's craftiness is to humbly acknowledge your own vulnerability to temptation and deception and to continually seek God's correction.

Ask God to search your heart, as David did in Psalm 139:23-24. "Search me, O God, and know my heart; test me and know my anxious thoughts. See if there is any offensive way in me, and lead me in the way everlasting."

This passage highlights three levels of knowledge. Only God knows your heart. Both God and you know your thoughts. God, you and all who see you know your ways. This hierarchy clearly illustrates the way that your hidden heart motives, which you cannot know unless God reveals them to you, can significantly impact your actions. Do not assume that your heart is pure. Remember Jeremiah 17:9: "The heart is deceitful above all things and beyond cure. Who can understand it?"

Be accountable to others

Finally, having a committed and open relationship with peers who will hold you accountable will enable you to finish well. You may be tempted, as you grow in ministry, to stop allowing others to hold you accountable. But you are only preparing yourself for a great fall.

No matter who you are, no matter how advanced and productive your leadership, you need people to hold you accountable. You need someone who will not personally benefit from your leadership decisions and who knows you well enough to ask, "How are you using your power?" "How is your devotional life?" "Are your thoughts under control?" Proverbs 11:14 says, "For lack of guidance a nation falls, but many advisers make victory sure." Proverbs 24:6 counsels, "for waging war you need guidance, and for victory many advisers."

---

[30] Maxwell, *The Leadership Bible*, commentary on Judges 12-16

CONCLUSION

Many people begin their service to God well. Few finish well. Receive the warnings of history, as evidenced in the lives of Uzziah, Solomon, and many other Biblical and contemporary leaders who fell terribly at the peak of their careers. Some made quite an impact; others simply disappeared into unimportance.

We know the story of David, who sinned terribly, paid a great price, repented, and received restoration. Leaders who have sinned should follow David's example and humbly repent so that God can restore them over time.

But you cannot approach sin lightly, for it brings great shame upon the name of God and great pain to others when leaders fall. Take great precautions to refuse the voice that says "You can enjoy this sin and then repent and be forgiven later." God knows your heart – He will see your casual dismissal of sin and He will know the sincerity of your repentance.

Finally, Peter, James, John, Paul and the contemporary leaders who have finished well can encourage you. It is possible. God provides a way out of every temptation. Be assured of His victory as you walk humbly with Him, never assuming that strength today assures victory tomorrow. My prayer is that both you and I will finish well.

ACTION ASSIGNMENT

1) Carefully read the following Scriptures, and put a mark beside them after reading.

_____ 2 Chronicles 26

_____ I Kings 3:1- 11:14

_____ Deuteronomy 17:14-20

_____ I Corinthians 9:24-27

_____ Philippians 3

2) Memorize 2 Timothy 4:7-8 and write it from memory.

3) Which of the thoughts below cross your mind when you think of becoming very successful in ministry?

(Acknowledging that certain thoughts have come to you does *not* indicate that they are your primary motivation. You are simply acknowledging, as a leader, that you have been tempted in these ways. This is the first step in guarding against them. Mark all that apply.)

_____ I like the feeling of leading under a powerful anointing

_____ I would like to be looked up to by others.

_____ I would like to prove to certain people that I can do it.

_____ The lifestyle of a big leader appeals to me.

_____ I would rather eat rich food and speak in many places, than do all the fasting, praying and seeking God that I have been doing.

_____ I would enjoy the privileges that accompany being a big leader.

4) Review the section "The Reasons Men Fall." Which one of the reasons most tempts to you at this point in your life and why?

5) Review the *Keys to Finish Well.* Which one is most needed in your life at this time? What will you do to put it into practice?

6) In what area did God most strongly speak to you through this lesson?

7) What steps will you now take, to assure that you will finish well? Be specific.

EPILOGUE

Congratulations, you've finished the book! Recognize, however, that God's work on your character is far from complete. His work is a life-long process of being "transformed into his likeness with ever-increasing glory, which comes from the Lord, who is the Spirit" (2 Corinthians 3:18). I pray, as you grow in your skills and ability to lead others, that God will keep your heart tender and open to His nurture and correction. He wants you, like David, to be a leader after His own heart. A right heart before God and a willingness to be used by Him creates a powerful combination through which you can accomplish great things for the kingdom of Christ.

> May the God of peace, who through the blood of the eternal covenant brought back from the dead our Lord Jesus, that great Shepherd of the sheep, equip you with everything good for doing his will, and may he work in us what is pleasing to him, through Jesus Christ, to whom be glory for ever and ever. Amen (Hebrews 13:20-21).

Recommended Books/Resources for Your Continued Growth

Anderson, Neil. *The Bondage Breaker.*

Barna, George, *The Power of Team Leadership.*

Blanchard, Ken et. al. *The Generosity Factor.*

Blanchard, Ken et. al. *Leadership by the Book.*

Blanchard, Ken. *The Heart of a Leader.*

Blanchard, Ken. *The Secret.*

Briner, Bob et al. *More Leadership Lessons of Jesus: A Timeless Model for Today's Leaders.*

Byler, *Use That Gift.*

Byler, *Authority.*

Byler, *7 Keys to Financial Freedom.*

Covey, Stephen. *The 7 Habits of Highly Effective People.*

Eims, LeRoy. *Be the Leader You Were Meant to Be.*

Finzel, Hans. *The Top 10 Mistakes Leaders Make.*

Finzel, Hans. *Empowered Leaders.*

Foster, Richard. *Celebration of Discipline.*

Hendricks, Howard. *Teaching to Change Lives.*

Hybels, Bill. *Courageous Leadership.* (Great book especially for pastors.)

Haggai, John Edmund. *Lead On!*

Hunter, Jim. *The Servant.*

Jacobs, Donald. *From Rubble to Rejoicing.*

James M. Kouzes, and Barry Z. Posner, *The Leadership Challenge*

LaHaye, Tim. *Why You Act the Way You Do.* (Great book for understanding yourself and others; explains the temperaments.)

Lencioni, Patrick. *The Five Dysfunctions of a Team.*

Littauer, Florence. *Personality Plus:How to Understand Others by Understanding Yourself.* (Great book on temperaments.)

MacDonald, Gordon. *Ordering Your Private World.*

Marshall, Tom. *Understanding Leadership.*

Maxwell, John C. and Donovan, Jim. *Becoming a Person of Influence.*

Maxwell, John C. *Developing the Leaders Around You.*

Maxwell, John C. *Developing the Leader Within You.*

Maxwell, *The Success Journey.*

Maxwell, *Failing Forward.*

Maxwell, *Priorities, the Pathway to Success.* (Video Presentation.)

Maxwell, *The 21 Irrefutable Laws of Leadership*

Maxwell, *There's No Such Thing As Business Ethics.*

Maxwell, *Partners in Prayer.* (A guide to developing a lay prayer ministry in the church.) See also the video, *The Pastor's MVP.*

Maxwell, *The 21 Most Powerful Minutes in a Leaders' Day.* (Biblical examples of the 21 Laws.)

Maxwell, *Thinking for a Change.*

Maxwell, *The Leadership Bible.* (Great Bible with all sorts of insights on leadership. NKJV and NIV)

Maxwell, *The Winning Attitude.*

Maxwell, *Injoy Life Club,* Leadership tape series. (Out of production but see web resources below for a site to find them.)

Meyer, Joyce. *Battlefield of the Mind.*

Meyer, Joyce. *How to Succeed at Being Yourself.*

Meyer, Joyce. *A Leader in the Making.*

Munroe, Myles. *Becoming a Leader.*

Munroe, Myles. *Understanding Your Potential.*

Pollock, David. *Church Administration the Dollars and Sense of it.*

Sanders, Oswald. *Spiritual Leadership.* (Classic reading on Christian leadership.)

Silvoso, Ed. *Anointed for Business.*

Smith, Ken. *It's About Time.* (Good book on time management.)

Swarr, Sharon. *Transform the World.* (Business and mission.)

Tennyson, Mack. *Church Finances for People Who Count.*

Veith, Gene. *God at Work* (On vocation.)

Warren, Rick. *The Purpose Driven Church.*

Warren, Rick. *The Purpose Driven Life.*

Wilkinson, Bruce. *The 7 Laws of the Learner.* (Excellent for Teachers. Also available as a video series.)

Wilkinson, Bruce, *Teaching with Style,* video series. (Excellent for teachers.)

Wilkinson, Bruce, *The Prayer of Jabez.*

Wilkinson, Bruce, *Secrets of the Vine.*

Wilkinson, Bruce, *The Dream Giver.*

Ziglar, Zig. *Over the Top.*

Ziglar, Zig. *Staying Up, Up, Up in a Down Down World.*

Web resources
(Visit the author's website for these links)

www.ncd-international.org, The home for Natural Church Development. They operate on the premise that a healthy church will grow and have tools to measure the health of a church in 8 key areas.
www.pastors.com, Rick Warren's Ministry ToolBox is a weekly newsletter full of tips, links, and articles to help you in your ministry. (also has many other resources for pastors, free sermons, etc.)
www.walkthru.org. Walk Through the Bible has many seminar and resources for training teachers
paul-timothy.net/ Training resources for pastors and church planters in multiple languages.
www.assess-yourself.org Free online tests to measure spiritual gifts, character, love for God, Worldview, and obstacles to growth.
www.lared.org A ministry devoted to teaching Biblical principles especially to business persons. Downloadable teaching material in PDF format and audio content.
www.world-map.com Provide free ACTS magazine and the book Shepherd's Staff to leaders in developing nations.
sgai.org/resources/audio/index.php Audio teachings by Malcolm Webber
www.highiqsociety.org/iq_tests/ Free intelligence test.
biblestudytools.com/ Free online Bible study tools and resources.
www.biblica.com Free online Bible and Bible study tools.
www.sermonillustrations.com/ Free sermon illustrations on a variety of topics.
www.searchgodsword.org/se/pbm/ Free Powerpoint Bible maps.
www.ebibleteacher.com/ Lots of clip art, pictures, maps and links to other resources.
www.xenos.org/ Vast amount of material from a church, podcasts, sermon notes, outlines, and theological papers.
www.ocafrica.net/ OC Africa publishes The Church Leader in Africa which can be viewed online.

Free email newsletters on leadership

Leadership Magazine. Free magazine by Pastor Gregg Johnson. Available in email format or hard copy, www.missionchurch.com/magazine/subscribe.htm Archived issues with excellent material are available at: www.acswebnetworks.com/leadershipmagazine/archives

Leadership Letters, free email letter by Malcolm Webber, www.LeadershipLetters.org

The Leadership Link, Resources and free email newsletter by Tim Elmore focused on young leaders. www.growingleaders.com

Leadership Wired, free email newsletter by John Maxwell and Pastor's Coach, free email newsletter by Dan Reiland. www.injoy.com/newsletters

Ministry ToolBox, a free weekly newsletter from Rick Warren full of tips, links, and articles to help you in your ministry. www.pastors.com

Reflections for Servant Leaders – biweekly ezine from Jon Byler on servant leadership. www.leadersserve.com

Bibliography

Clay, Henry. *Text-Book of Eloquence, a Collection of Axioms, Apothegms, Sentiments, Gathered from the Public Speeches of Henry Clay.* Edited by G. Vandenhoff. n.p., 1844.

Byler, Jon. *Free at Last.* Nairobi Kenya: Centre for Christian Discipleship, 1997.

Franklin, Benjamin. *Poor Richard's Almanac,* 1734. n.p., n.d.

Habecker, Eugene B. *Rediscovering the Soul of Leadership.* Colorado Springs, CO: Victor Books, 1996.

Hession, Roy. *The Calvary Road.* Fort Washington, PA: CLC Publications, 1964.

Houston, Tom. *King David.* n.p.: MARC Europe, 1987.

Maxwell, John C. *Developing the Leader Within You.* Nashville, TN: Thomas Nelson, 1993.

Maxwell, John C. "Leadership That Goes the Distance." *Leadership Wired.* 3.9 (April 2000).

Maxwell, John C. *The 21 Indispensable Qualities of a Leader.* Nashville, TN: Nelson Business, 1999.

Maxwell, John C. *The Success Journey.* Nashville, TN: Nelson Business, 1997.

McMillen, S.I., and David E. Stern. *None of These Diseases,* revised ed. Grand Rapids, MI.: Fleming H. Revell, 2000.

Mnkandla, Ngwiza. *The Church Leader in Africa,* 4th Qtr. 2000.

Munroe, Myles. *Becoming a Leader, Everyone Can Do It.* Bakersfield, CA: Pneuma Life, 1993.

Nee, Watchman. *Release of the Spirit,* reissue ed. Richmond, VA: Christian Fellowship Publishers, 2000.

Toler, Stan. *Minute Motivators.* Colorado Springs, CO: River Oak Publishing, 2002.

Renner, Rick. *Who Is Ready for a Spiritual Promotion?* Tulsa, OK: Rick Renner Ministries, 2000.

Sanders, J. Oswald. *Spiritual Leadership.* Chicago: Moody Press, 1994.

Smalley, Gary. *If Only He Knew.* Grand Rapids, MI.: Zondervan, 1982.

About the Author

Jon Byler has a passion to serve the body of Christ by using his gifts of teaching, writing and encouragement. He especially enjoys serving the leaders who build the church. He lives with his wife, Loice in East Petersburg, PA. USA. Together they pastor an emerging church and are the parents of three children.

Jon served in Kenya for 13 years and in different capacities in the church including pastoral ministry and leadership development. He has authored several books including *7 Keys to Financial Freedom*, *The Heart of Christian Leadership* and *The Art of Christian Leadership*, and several booklets on other topics. He writes a bi-weekly e-Zine *Reflections for Servant Leaders* which is distributed by email in English and Spanish. (Sign up to receive a free copy on his website.) Jon is available for speaking and consulting especially in the areas of leadership, church growth, and missions. For more information see his website, www.LeadersServe.com. He currently serves as the LEAD Director for Global Disciples, a ministry committed to assisting churches around the world train their own disciples, church planters and leaders. For more information about Global Disciples visit www.GlobalDisciples.org.

Made in the USA
Monee, IL
17 September 2021

78295297R00111